COMBAT LEGEND

REPUBLIC
P-47
THUNDERBOLT

Jerry Scutts

Airlife

Copyright © 2003 The Crowood Press Ltd

Text written by Jerry Scutts
Profile illustrations drawn by Dave Windle
Cover painting by Jim Brown – The Art of Aviation Co. Ltd

First published in the UK in 2003
by Airlife Publishing, an imprint of The Crowood Press Ltd

British Library Cataloguing-in-Publication Data
A catalogue record for this book
is available from the British Library

ISBN 1 84037 402 0

Printed in Malaysia

*Contact us for a free catalogue that describes the complete range of Airlife
books for pilots and aviation enthusiasts.*

Airlife Publishing
An imprint of The Crowood Press Ltd
Ramsbury, Marlborough, Wiltshire SN8 2HR
E-mail: enquiries@crowood.com

www.crowood.com

Contents

Thunderbolt Timeline

P-47C-2 (41-6264) was one of the first Thunderbolts to reach England in the spring of 1943. *(IWM)*

6 May 1941
Test pilot Lowery Brabham makes the maiden fight of the XP-47B

8 August 1942
Prototype XP-47B lost in crash

8 April 1943
Combat debut of P-47 with 8th Air Force in England

15 April 1943
First P-47 aerial victory in European theatre by the 4th Fighter Group

29 June 1943
Capt Charles London of the 78th Fighter Group becomes the first 8th Air Force P-47 ace

3 July 1943
Bubble canopy conversion of XP-47K completed

16 August 1943
The 358th Fighter Group enters combat as the first P-47 unit in the Pacific Area of Operations

11 October 1943
Lt Col Neel Kearby, CO of the 348th Fighter Group destroys six Japanese aircraft to win the Medal of Honor, the first bestowed on an AAF fighter pilot in WWII

5 August 1944
Record speed of 505 mph (812.7 km/h) claimed for the XP-47J (43-6952); AAF figures verify a speed of 493 mph (793.4 km/h)

14 September 1944
No 261 Squadron flies first RAF Thunderbolt sortie in the Far East

20 September 1944
Aviatrix Jacqueline Cochran names 10,000th Thunderbolt *Ten Grand* in ceremony at Farmingdale.

25 April 1945
Lt Raymond Knight of the 350th Fighter Group in Italy is awarded a posthumous Medal of Honor for attempting to save his crippled P-47

July 1945
Farmingdale rolls out *Fifteen Grand* – 5,000 more P-47s having been built since completing P-47D named *Ten Grand* the previous September

26 July 1945
First flight of the first XP-47H (42-23297)

9 Nov 1945
Republic completes P-47N-25-RE (44-89450), the last of 15,660 P-47s built

31 October 1950
Only known armed action by US Air National Guard F-47Ns, when Thunderbolts are used to help quell unrest in Puerto Rico

18–30 June 1954
Last-known armed action by Republic Thunderbolts when F-47Ns are used to support the CIA-backed operation to depose Guatemalan president Jacabo Arbenz

1. Republic P-47 Thunderbolt: Prototypes and Development

The evolution of the Republic P-47 Thunderbolt showed a fortuitous adherence to tried and tested principles of fighter design at a time when the United States Army Air Corps was prepared to look at any number of innovative ideas, particularly radical airframes. The problem with some of these was that they were not only very advanced and complex, they were often drawn up around powerplants that were not proven and in some cases, not even built. Had such aircraft been funded and the airframe or engine installation failed for some reason or other, the government could have been in a very critical position in regard to the first-line aircraft it subsequently needed for combat in World War II. As it was, the United States found itself short of world-class fighters when the country suddenly became a combatant on 7 December 1941. Fortunately manufacturers such as the Republic Aviation Corporation of Long Island, New York, had been working to redress that deficit.

Seversky Aircraft, the Republic forerunner until October 1939, had traditionally designed fighters with radial engines but it looked to principal US engine supplier Allison as a possible source of liquid-cooled power for several fighter designs dramatically different to the company's previous efforts. One was the AP-12 Rocket which featured a buried engine – a popular but misguided pre-war principal which might have proved difficult to perfect. Another, in keeping with a liquid- rather than air-cooled theme, was the XP-47A.

Although this latter sounds like the logical forerunner of the Thunderbolt, it was also Allison-powered and bore more resemblance to the Curtiss P-40 than the familiar Republic fighter. Only one full scale mock-up of the XP-47A was completed before chief engineer Alexander Kartveli turned his attention to a larger, revised design known as the XP-47B. In its turn this concept leant heavily on the P-44-1 Warrior, a fighter very similar to the P-47 and which was on the point of being manufactured for the Air Corps to meet an order for 80 aircraft placed on 13 September 1940.

Turbocharged power

Kartveli's insistence that the P-44-1 would prove to be underpowered and virtually obsolete by the time it entered service persuaded the AAC to await a revised design. This, initially known as the P-44-2, would be a vast improvement thanks to a turbo-supercharger and fuel enough for a substantial range. But even these changes did not satisfy Kartveli who returned to his drawing board to make further revisions. This time he turned a Republic P-43 Lancer clone, via the P-44, into the P-47. Pratt & Whitney's R-2800 radial promised an output of 2,000 hp, a dramatic increase in power over what had gone before.

The conception of the XP-47 fitted with the most powerful radial engine then available was very different to the original proposal for an extremely lightweight fighter powered by a liquid-cooled engine. Estimated to have weighed 4,900 lb (2223 kg), a figure comparing favourably with that of the later P-51 at 8,633 lb

An outgrowth of the Seversky 1XP and 2XP, the latter in turn being similar to the 3XAR, the P-35A entered USAAC service by default when a Swedish export order was taken over after Pearl Harbor. (*Republic*)

(3916 kg) the Allison-engined proposal had dimensions comparable to other fighters of the day. The actual XP-47 was just the opposite.

Kartveli, realising that the configuration he envisaged for the XP-47 would prove too small for the R-2800, then designed a larger aircraft under the designation XP-47B. It was fortunate indeed that Kartveli stayed with the R-2800 for this became what was in the opinion of many the best radial aero-engine ever built.

On 13 September 1940, some four months before the prototype first flew, the Air Corps placed an order for 773 P-47s on the strength of the company's projected figures for the revised design. Worth $56 million to Republic, the inital contract covered 171 P-47Bs and 602 P-47Cs and was the largest order the US government had ever placed for fighter aircraft.

Following the successful first flight of the XP-47B in the hands of Lowery Brabham on 6 May 1941, some further design changes were made, the most externally obvious being the deletion of the 'car door'-type cockpit entry on the first four P-47s. Early that year Republic's Director of Military Contracts, C Hart Miller had named the P-47 'Thunderbolt'.

For the rest of 1941 Republic worked steadily to complete the initial AAC order, the company completing the first P-47B for Army acceptance

trials on 21 December. Air tests determined both average and maximum performance figures for the new fighter which, in the calm of pre-war Long Island, appeared highly encouraging. The P-47 out-performed both its contemporaries, the P-39 Airacobra and Curtiss P-40, with relative ease, despite being larger and heavier than any single-engined US fighter that had gone before it.

Construction

The P-47's fuselage was a semi-monocoque all-metal structure with a stressed skin built in upper and lower sections, split horizontally and bolted together. The tail was built as a complete section for attachment to the fuselage. Four quick-release panels formed the engine cowling, fastened to support rings attached to the engine valve rocker covers. These also incorporated hydraulically-operated ventilation flaps.

The main fuel tank, holding 250 US gallons (208 Imp gal/946 l), was situated below the cockpit, with a second tank holding 100 US gals (83.3 Imp gal/378.5 l) located directly aft of the rear wing hinge support bulkheads.

A General Electric exhaust-driven turbo-supercharger was situated about 21 feet (6.4 m) behind the propeller and connected to the engine by internal, lower fuselage trunking. This trunking, which helped dictate the large size of the aircraft, fed air for supercharging from an intake at the lower lip of the engine cowling through an intercooler and back along either side of the fuselage to the single carburettor intake.

The lower forward fuselage incorporated small exhaust ports intended to discharge gases not required for turbo power. Large exhaust waste gates were built into both sides of the fuselage aft of the wing. All this internal plumbing led to a plethora of cockpit instrumentation that was quite daunting to pilots new to the P-47. But once they became familiar with the function of the controls the workload was found not to be the mammoth task it may have seemed.

Many of the turbo functions were linked so that few separate pilot actions were required. Above all, build quality was the keynote of the P-47; and for the first time a US fighter had

been given an armament that would prove to be more than adequate in combat.

Natural hazard

With fighter speeds nudging 400 mph (644 km/h) in level flight, test pilots began to experience severe buffeting when new aircraft such as the P-47 were put into a vertical dive. As speed built up they found that the controls stiffened up, sometimes to the point of feeling as though they were locked solid. Little was really understood as to why this phenomenon occurred or how it could be overcome, so the term compressibility was used to cover the most obvious effects. That it could seriously – and adversely – affect the performance of high-speed combat aircraft was obvious but no easy solution appeared to present itself apart from informing pilots and posting 'never exceed' warning notices in the cockpit.

Both the P-47 and P-38 experienced the effects of compressibility and a number of

First flown in 1941, the P-43 Lancer was a progenitor of the P-47, with a similar wing planform and a turbocharger. It was also the first US fighter to exceed 300 mph. (*Republic*)

Devoid of any identifying markings, the bare 'natural metal finish' (NMF) of the Republic XP-47B was typical of US military protoypes of the early 1940s. National insignia were soon applied. (*Republic*)

pilots died as a direct result of several early examples of these aircraft breaking up (the tail coming off in the P-47's case) when they were dived too steeply. In the event of the aircraft becoming almost uncontrollable, a pilot's natural tendency to haul back on the stick to achieve pull-out was often to no avail. In that instance the stresses imposed on the airframe invariably proved too great, leading to control-surface damage and occasionally catastrophic failure and pilot fatality.

Fortunately, enough pilots did manage to return to earth after such wild flights for stress engineers to examine fabric-covered control surfaces shredded by the effects of near-transonic airflow. An inkling of what the pilot had experienced was gained, but in any case very little remedial action appeared to be possible.

Republic limited the dive speed of the P-47 to 500 mph (804.7 km/h) IAS at altitudes up to 25,000 ft (7620 m) and to 400 mph (644 km/h) above that height. It was recommended that dive recovery be initiated no lower than at 12,000 ft (3658 m). At that altitude the P-47's dive speed limit corresponded to 601 mph (967.2 km/h) TAS and a Mach number of 0.82, when the aircraft was well into a compressibility condition. Then it took on a drag coefficient of at least two and a half times what it was at more moderate speeds.

Not until after the war was it appreciated that only 'clean' turbojet aircraft could achieve supersonic flight (760 mph or 1223 km/h at sea level) with relative ease. Until then, breaking the so-called 'sound barrier' represented a dangerous build-up of 'solid' air which no aircraft powered by a reciprocating engine could penetrate.

Transonic in a dive

Despite that, there were instances during the war where several pilots were actually credited with flying the P-47 transonically, among them Cass Hough of 8th Air Force Service Command. Republic had claimed much the same achievement as early as 1 December 1942 when a press release stated that two Army pilots had dived their P-47Bs to at least 725 mph (1167 km/h). Publicity of that kind did the company no harm, but it was clearly quite optimistic and bent some fundamental laws of aeronautics.

With Thunderbolt pilot training programmes emphasising the danger of ignoring steep dive angles and speed limit warnings, this problem did not manifest itself very often during the

Among the early Thunderbolts tested at Wright Field was this P-47B (41-5931), part of the initial production batch of 171 aircraft. The white number was a Wright Field application. (*IWM*)

conflict and never to the point where combat operations were dangerously compromised. Compressibility and its effects nevertheless remain a part of P-47 lore – but in the event few major airframe modifications were found to be necessary to offset the possible adverse effects of it. In the meantime some sort of automatic brake on diving speed was an obvious solution and Republic set about developing what turned out to be a pair of underwing dive flaps that appeared on late-production P-47Ds.

Combat-worthy

Aerodynamics aside, the designers of the 'second generation' of US monoplane fighters faced other challenges. Republic had been informed about some of them in February 1940 and in May an Air Corps special board convened to look into the quality of US fighter design and combat suitability in the light of reports from the war in Europe. These included a catalogue of vital items that military aircraft would henceforth need to survive against the best Axis fighters. Far from alone in being unable at that time to field aircraft that demonstrated an amalgam of engine power, good performance, protection for the pilot, adequate armament and other vital attributes,

American engineers set themselves the task of finding a remedy for this serious lack.

Among the items of military equipment needed by modern fighters were self-sealing fuel tanks, heavier-calibre and in many cases a greater number of guns, pilot oxygen equipment, bad-weather navigational aids, and so on. American radio communications had traditionally been HF 'command, transmit and receive' sets used in conjunction with ground stations; these had to be adaptable to international rather than simply US domestic standards.

Because the country might soon be at war – although this was by no means certain in 1940 – American aircraft designers strove to match world standards.

Alexander Kartveli had estimated that such changes to the XP-47 would add some 250 lb (113 kg) and delay the completion of the prototype for 60 days. But the work had to be done; even though the lessons of combat flying were not entirely new to US fighters at that time, they stemmed mainly from figures garnered by a motley collection of obsolescent designs despatched to China to assist in her war with Japan. Republic's own P-43 Lancer and the Seversky forerunner, the P-35, had been

9

A photograph that well illustrates the 'high' termination of the cowling flaps on the early razorback P-47s. S/n 41-6403 was one of 362 P-47C-5s. (*MAP*)

sold abroad, and before long types such as the Curtiss P-36 and Bell P-39 were being ordered by European powers. The prospect of aerial combat with German aircraft was viewed as a significant raising of the stakes due to the much-publicised technical superiority of the *Luftwaffe*.

Production P-47B

The first P-47B (41-5895) was completed in December 1941 and despatched to Wright Field for use by the AAF as a pattern test aircraft for the type. The four following aircraft completed in March 1942 were also used for tests although the last example (41-5899) crashed on the 26th, killing Republic test pilot George Burrell. The cause was found to be loss of part of the tail assembly as a result of compressibility.

Examination of the wreckage revealed that fabric on the elevators had 'ballooned' under extreme pressure and caused loss of control. On 1 May Joe Parker, another of Republic's test pilots, experienced much the same effect but he managed to bail out leaving the sixth P-47B (41-5900) to its fate in the waters of Long Island Sound.

Republic tested a contra-rotating propeller on a 'C'-type engine fitted in P-47B 41-5942, C Hart Miller himself making the proving flights.

At the time, little publicity was given to this modification, known to the company as the 'double twister'. The aircraft was apparently something of a handful to fly as the contra-rotating propeller induced zero torque. In effect it neutralised the action of the offset vertical stabiliser that all P-47s carried to counteract torque, and was quite unstable.

The new propeller, fitted to the all-yellow P-47B, was photographed by Republic's AAF plant representative, Major Russell Keillor. Flight test results were quietly shelved until presumably being used during the final design of the XP-72, which was fitted with a contra-rotating propeller. Later, a further series of propeller tests took place, utilising a P-47D. The aircraft was fitted with a Curtiss unit with curved, scimitar-shaped blades the tips of which rotated at supersonic speeds.

In regard to standard P-47s, Republic decided that a metal-covered rudder and elevators would be fitted as soon as time allowed but in the meantime the first delivery of B models to the Army was made, on 26 May 1941. These aircraft had the original fabric-covered control surfaces.

It was as a result of the apprehension over further enemy attack after 7 December that the 56th Fighter Group was moved from Carolina

Although RAF squadrons did not receive Thunderbolts until 1944, the Aeroplane & Armament Experimental Establishment at Boscombe Down tested several early models, including this P-47D-1 (52-7922) borrowed from 8th Air Force stocks. (*via Tim Mason*)

to the vicinity of the Republic plant. This made it convenient to allocate the first Thunderbolts to the 56th, along with the 80th, a newly formed fighter group. For their part the AAF pilots became unofficial company test pilots and rapidly built up flight experience in a training programme that encompassed a fair degree of technical troubleshooting.

Mastering a fighter that was radically different to anything they had previously flown gave the young Army pilots quite a challenge. Several members of the 56th paid with their lives while attempting to take the aircraft to its performance limits, the exuberance of youth resulting in an embarrassing log of wrecked and damaged P-47s. Further urgent notices went out to restrict the diving speed to 300 mph (482.8 km/h) and an embargo was placed on violent manoeuvres and aerobatics.

Some of the 'crack-ups' had their positive side. Thoroughly aware that not only was the P-47 the biggest and heaviest fighter they had ever flown, pilots were equally amazed at its strength. The fact that it would protect them well in a crash-landing that could wreck the aircraft – not to mention most objects in its path – was highly appreciated.

By September 1942 Republic had handed over the first P-47Cs to the Army. Despite remedial modifications, the new Thunderbolts continued to fall out of the sky as a result of control loss at excessive air speeds. With only an elevator trim tab and engine power to pull the big fighter out of a high-speed dive, pilots were again advised to monitor their performance and avoid approaching anywhere near the P-47's terminal velocity of about 600 mph. A major change to the P-47C-1 was to lengthen the fuselage by 8 inches (20.3 cm) forward of the firewall, to improve flight characteristics by shifting the centre of gravity. This increased fuselage length to just over 36 feet (10.97 m). Other detail improvements were made, these being mostly 'under the skin'. Two further P-47C model production blocks representing 490 aircraft were completed before a designation change was made.

P-47D

Incorporating the progressive changes made to the P-47C, the first four D models built at Evansville retained the 'razorback' fuselage and had, among other changes, metal-covered rudder and elevators. These and other detail changes to the landing gear, supercharger air ducting, hydraulics and electrics had been incorporated on the first P-47C-1 (41-6066) which acted in effect as a prototype, mainly to

To test the 'all-round-vision' concept, a British Typhoon canopy was modified to fit the cut-down rear fuselage spine of the last P-47D-5 (42-8702). This conversion became the sole P-47K in July 1943. (*Republic*)

The TP-47G from Curtiss production was an elaborate design exercise which involved moving the front cockpit forward. Combat units put a second seat behind the standard cockpit of the P-47D with far less engineering work. Only two two-seat Thunderbolts were built, the actual conversions almost certainly being undertaken by Republic. (*Republic*)

check out the revised fuselage configuration for the succeeding model.

Alexander Kartveli's views on P-47 modifications such as extra fuel tanks, wing racks and so forth, were quite negative. He had to be convinced to fit a reinforced keel to the P-47D's lower fuselage in order to accommodate hardpoints for drop tanks, but these would not appear until later, on the P-47D-15.

Curtiss was contracted to share in P-47 production and built 354 aircraft at its Buffalo, New York plant. Used primarily as trainers in the US, two G models were fitted out as two-seaters by installing a second cockpit and

moving the front one forwards by several feet. No production was undertaken, but there were two-seat Thunderbolts in combat zones, the ingenuity of groundcrews extending to converting 'war weary' aircraft. In those instances the second seat was installed behind the standard cockpit of the P-47D, space being made for a second seat by removing radio and oxygen equipment. The 56th Group also used a two-seat P-47D-11 conversion (42-75276) on four operational sorties, the aircraft's role being to detect enemy aircraft using AN/APM-19 *Rosebud* S-band radar.

One P-47G (42-24964) was used by Wright Field in 1944 to test a fixed landing gear fitted with skis. This was part of wide-ranging series of tests to determine the feasibility of fighters operating from snow-covered airfields. No production of skis was undertaken.

The Curtiss P-47 line at Buffalo closed in March 1944. It had taken an unacceptable year

Kokomo, alias P-47D-25 42-26637, was on 25 March 1945 the personal mount of 2nd Air Division CO, Maj Gen William Kepner. The nose badge is that of IV Fighter Command, which Kepner took over in February 1942 before coming to England in 1943. Note the AAF 'stars and bars' on the inner wheel hub covers. (*USAF*)

and a half to complete 354 aircraft, and a further 4,220 P-47Gs were cancelled.

Improved pilot vision

With numerous razorback P-47Ds in service ground crews attempted to improve the pilots' view directly aft. Various methods were tried including side panels with a prominent clear perspex bubble in place of the standard 'greenhouse' panels. Much admired was the British Malcolm hood, a blown, frameless section which replaced the sliding canopy on the P-47 and the 'flip up, flip down' windows on the P-51B. The Malcolm hood found its way onto a relatively small number of Thunderbolts as AAF Mustang pilots seem to have made a better case for those that were available. There were never really enough Malcolm hoods to go around as RAF Mustang IIIs had first call on them.

The most satisfactory solution to the visual restrictions of the early-model P-47 was the introduction of a full bubbletop hood. Up to the P-47D-23, progressive models of Thunderbolt

retained the original highback or 'razorback' fuselage, but the installation of an all-round-vision canopy was to bring about the first major design revision of the Thunderbolt with the P-47D-25 production block.

After completing the modification of the last P-47D-5-RE (42-8702) to take a Hawker Typhoon canopy by 3 July 1943, this aircraft was flight tested as the sole XP-47K. Cutting down the rear fuselage aft of the cockpit induced some loss of stability and Republic subsequently designed a thin dorsal fin to restore flight characteristics. First supplied for retro-fitting as a field kit, the dorsal fin was not introduced on production aircraft until the P-47D-40 and by no means all earlier aircraft were so modified. It appears, as with many mass-produced machines, that individual aircraft differed enough for the loss of keel stability to be pronounced in only some examples.

Regarding the new bubble canopy the phrase 'all-round-vision' needed some qualification. Pilots certainly enjoyed 360-degree vision once the aircraft was airborne, and few disputed that

The second YP-47M (42-23786) running up to full power. Its bright yellow cowling indicates that this is a Republic test aircraft, flown at the time of the photo by company test pilot Mike Ritchie. (*Republic*)

the new canopy greatly improved visibility to each side and directly aft compared to the old 'greenhouse' type. But the massive bulk of the engine still masked the view directly forward on the ground, so much so that a groundcrewman riding on the wing and directing the pilot by hand signals became necessary on some of the makeshift airfields the P-47 used. A wheel 'in the rough' could easily lead to a bogged-down aircraft and a partially- or fully-blocked runway, causing serious disruption of mission schedules.

In the air a very tall pilot flying a P-47D-25 had other problems. The rudder pedals were only adjustable so far, and some individuals were obliged to sit higher in the cockpit than they would have preferred. Legend has it that some pilots, unable to bear this acute feeling of nakedness and vulnerability acquired 'canopy curtains', probably in the form of the standard blind-flying hood designed for the bubbletops. Working on the principle of the softtop fitted to a convertible car, the hood went together via a set of flexible rods, eyebolts and a canvas cover.

This model of the P-47 also introduced a flat cockpit windscreen to replace the original pointed screen fitted with internal armour glass, which had been standard on razorback models of the Thunderbolt.

Other, less obvious improvements to the P-47D-25 included an increase in internal main fuel tankage to 270 US gal (225 Imp gal/1022 l), and in water tank capacity, to 30 gal (25 Imp gal/113.6 l). With the water-injection 'on' the R-2800-59 coupled to a Hamilton Standard Hydromatic paddle-bladed propeller received an extra power boost which was highly appreciated by combat pilots. These features turned the P-47 into an aerial fighter equal to the best the *Luftwaffe* could put into the air.

Dive recovery flaps

The previously mentioned dive recovery flaps were introduced on the final P-47D-40 production models. Fitted forward of each inboard flap section, these hinged plates extended up to 22 degrees and helped break up the airflow to prevent any dangerous build-up of pressure and 'freezing' of the control surfaces. They worked extremely well according to reports, recovery being almost automatic at all altitudes. Furthermore, there was no resulting structural danger to the aircraft, despite the fact that upon initiating recovery by deploying the flaps at 25,000 to 27,000 ft (7620/8230 m) the pilot was pulling about 4.5 G. This rose to around 6 G at 17,000 ft (5182 m) and fell to 3 G at 1,000 ft (305 m) due

As the fin logo says, this was the single XP-47N prototype, which incorporated enough modifications to make it significantly different to the P-47D. Lowery Brabham is in the cockpit. (*MAP*)

to a natural tendency for the aircraft to pull out of compressibility at lower altitudes.

P-47M and P-47N

Republic fitted the R-2800-14W and -57 engines in the trio of D-27 models that became YP-47Ms, the latter powerplant giving out up to 2,800 hp for short periods. Otherwise known as the 'C' Series engine, this could haul the Thunderbolt along at a maximum of 473 mph (761.2 km/h) and proved ideal for the last direct derivative of the D model. It was decided that all 130 P-47Ms built would go to the 56th Fighter Group in the UK and the aircraft were prepared for shipping. The first examples arrived in January 1944.

Unfortunately a whole catalogue of engine troubles occurred not unlike those suffered by the first P-47s in England. After months of frustrating work the problem was solved by changing every engine.

While addressing the range shortcomings of the later-model P-47Ds, Republic initiated a significant redesign as the XP-47N. Based on a P-47D-27, 42-27387, the prototype was virtually a P-47M fitted with a new wing. Compared to the familiar elliptical wing of earlier Thunderbolts, the line of the trailing edge had been straightened and the tips clipped. The

landing-gear track was increased to more than 18 feet (5.49 m) and although the fuselage length remained as before, a fin fillet deeper than fitted to late-model Ds was introduced as a production item.

For the first time a P-47 was given what was later known as a 'wet' wing, internal tankage consisting of four fuel cells containing 200 US gallons (166.5 Imp gal/757 l). Progressive changes produced six production blocks of the P-47N, such items as zero-length rocket launchers being introduced on the N-5 and more efficient bomb racks and improved K-14 gunsights on the N-15. At more than seven tons all-up weight, the P-47N could be a handful to get off the ground especially when fully laden with bombs, rockets and drop tanks. However, those tanks plus internal fuel gave it one of the longest reaches of any wartime fighter, the P-47N-1 having a normal range of 800 miles (1287 km) and a maximum of 2,000 miles (3219 km) at 25,000 ft (7620 m).

Experimental Thunderbolts

There were several attempts by Republic to improve the P-47's performance and general capability by modifying the standard airframe. The first started life as a P-47B (41-6065) and was fitted with a pressure cabin. The aircraft

A design exercise that did not lead to any changes to standard production Thunderbolts was the introduction of cabin pressurisation. The single P-47B (41-6065) equipped in this way is seen here. (*Republic*)

was unarmed and initially had a performance similar to a standard B model. Although this was subsequently improved upon during a lengthy test programme, no other pressurised P-47s were built.

A second P-47B (41-5938) was used in tests of a laminar-flow wing. No armament was fitted and the mainplane was entirely redesigned, the familiar elliptical planform being replaced by a straight taper on leading and trailing edges. With a span over two feet (61 cm) longer than standard, the XP-47E was purely experimental, no production being contemplated. The aircraft existed until 14 October 1943 when it was destroyed in a crash that claimed the life of pilot Captain A McAdams.

After Republic's own test pilots had checked out each new version of the P-47 it was the turn of the Air Force. At Wright Field all significant modifications made to an established type had to be examined and officially approved, irrespective of whether or not they would appear on service aircraft. The test team at Wright flew many Thunderbolt sorties during the war years and, invariably, there were incidents and accidents.

Most dramatically different to the configuration of any standard Thunderbolt was the Chrysler-engined XP-47H (42-23297) which originated as a Republic-built P-47D-15 airframe. The next D-15 off the production line (42-23298) was also allocated for the installation of the 2,500 hp XI-2220-11 inverted-vee liquid-cooled engine. This gave the aircraft a pointed nose over two feet longer than a standard D model. Redesigned forward of the firewall, the H model had a General Electric CH-05 supercharger installed and was a conversion intended purely as an engine test-bed rather than an attempt to improve the performance of the Thunderbolt.

Geared powerplant

The XI-2220 was designed to obtain 2,000 hp from a liquid-cooled powerplant by transferring power from the crankshaft to the propeller shaft via a series of gears, the shaft itself being buried between the cylinder banks. Before it flew the engine attained 2,500 hp during its 50-hour test phase.

The first XP-47H made its maiden flight on 26 July 1945 and testing continued after the end of the war. On its twenty-seventh flight during November the aircraft suffered a broken

A single P-47D was fitted with the immensely powerful Pratt & Whitney R-2800-61 engine. The aircraft, designated as the XP-47J, was the first aircraft to fly at over 500 mph. (*Republic*)

propeller shaft and the pilot was forced to make a dead-stick landing. By then the need for new high-performance piston engines was greatly reduced thanks to the development of the jet, and the second aircraft was not completed.

The single XP-47J (43-46952) was a D-model airframe with doctored nose contours incorporating an engine-cooling fan under a shortened cowling, a propeller spinner and various components that were redesigned to be lighter than standard. As with any comparable test programme, the gains had to be significant enough to warrant some inevitable disruption of production lines to produce a new version. In the case of the XP-47J they were not and no such modifications were introduced.

Speed and climb tests

However, testing had its moments. In August 1943 Ralph Hoewing, a Wright Field test pilot and engineer, was sent to complete time-to-climb and speed tests on the XP-47J. With water injection the aircraft's P&W R-2800-61 produced 3,000 hp on take-off. The extra power enabled the test P-47 to climb well to its assigned altitude of about 36,000 ft (10970 m).

Standard procedure was for a speed run to last three to four minutes at a given power setting, which gave an accurate airspeed

reading. Hoewing began the run but had to terminate it after the engine lost power – directly above New York's Central Park. After an emergency landing at Farmingdale the aircraft was re-engined and Hoewing tried again. This time the engine blew before the speed run could be completed, a doubly annoying occurrence since the pilot noted his speed as close on 500 mph (804.7 km/h). Trailing smoke and with zero oil pressure Hoewing put the XP-47J down once more. Another engine change was made for a further flight 48 hours later. With a fair idea of the correct power setting for the high-speed run, Hoewing attained it and made the run – just before the engine failed. On landing, the prop stopped completely.

But the data had been obtained: the XP-47J's true airspeed was logged at 506 mph (814.3 km/h) in level flight. An outstanding feat for any aircraft in 1943, the record stood for some years until broken by the early turbojets. The speed was kept secret at the time, on the grounds that few people would have believed it. Ralph Hoewing himself knows that he inadvertently set another record – three flights, three engine failures and three engine changes!

At various times through WWII, various models of P-47 were assigned to the National

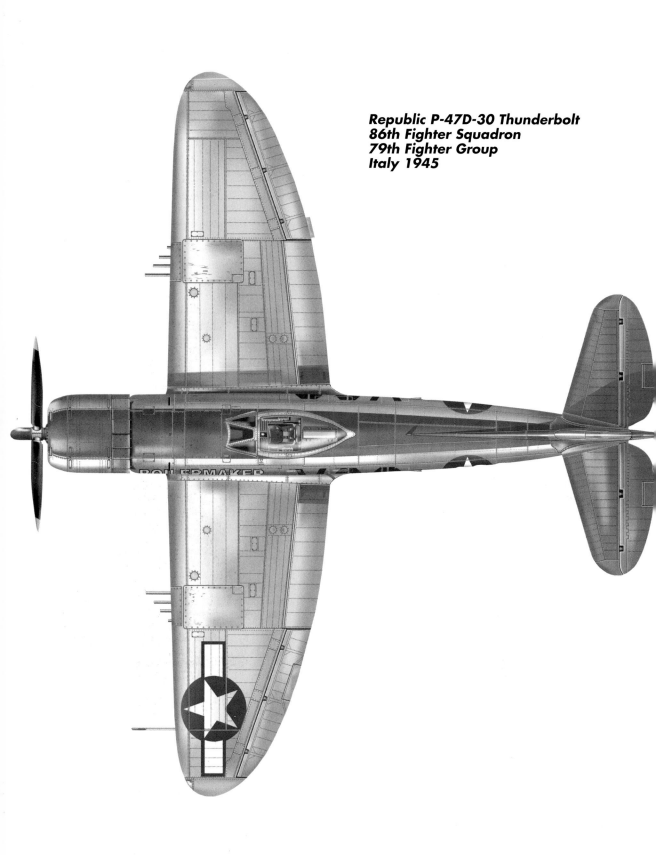

Republic P-47D-30 Thunderbolt
86th Fighter Squadron
79th Fighter Group
Italy 1945

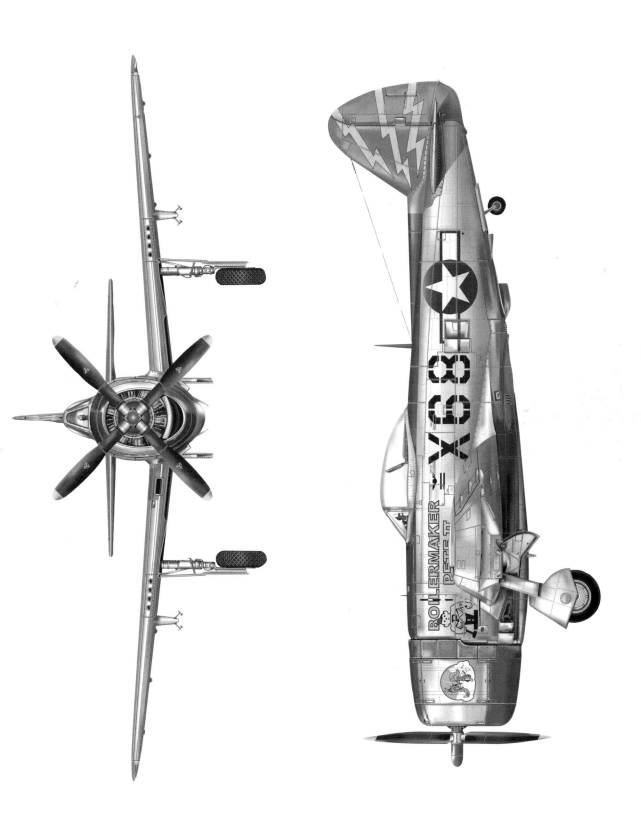

The last and arguably most aesthetically pleasing derivative of the P-47 was the XP-72. Very fast and heavily armed, it surely would have seen considerable service had WWII continued into 1946. (*Republic*)

Advisory Committee for Aeronautics (NACA) test centres located at Ames, California; Langley, Virginia; and Lewis, Ohio. Thunderbolts from the XP-47B through to the N were the subject of various flight programmes aimed at increasing their suitability as combat aircraft. Even those examples not seriously considered for front-line service furthered the advance of aeronautical knowledge. Such tests involved all categories of aircraft and all design aspects including powerplants. To take just two examples: P-47G 42-24929 was only the second aircraft to arrive at the new Lewis Centre in January 1943 to determine radial engine and supercharger performance. Late in the war, in June 1945, P-47N-1 44-88282 was used in a three-month test to reduce fuel boil-off during the climb-out phase of flight. In between, the P-47 had become a familiar sight at all three of NACA's facilities.

Ultimate Thunderbolt

Finally (numerically at least) there was the XP-72. As a result of fitting a new Pratt & Whitney R-4360-13 engine, the 3,500 hp Wasp Major, Republic allocated a new model number as the XP-72's configuration was dramatically different to the standard aircraft. A new fuselage the same length as that of the P-47D incorporated a bubble canopy and a ventral supercharger air intake in line with the wing

leading edge. This allowed the characteristic cowling scoop intake and rear fuselage waste gates of the P-47 to be dispensed with. With its 28 cylinders the engine was the most powerful brought to production status during WWII.

Two XP-72 concept aircraft (43-6598 and 43-6599) were built. Designed to drive a contra-rotating Aero Products propeller, the first example flew instead with a conventional four-blade unit, on 2 February 1944. Test pilot Carl Bellinger clocked up a true air speed of 489 mph (787 km/h) on an early test flight.

The contra-prop was ready for the second aircraft which made its maiden flight that same month. Six rather than eight machine guns armed the XP-72, production versions of which were planned to be armed with four 37-mm cannon plus two 1,000-lb (454-kg) bombs. Performance tests showed that the XP-72 was capable of a top speed of 490 mph (789 km/h) at 25,000 feet (7620 m) and had a normal range of 1,200 miles (1931 km).

The specification impressed the AAF enough for an order for 100 examples to be placed, but anticipated disruption of the Thunderbolt production line was one of the factors that quickly saw the order switched in favour of the less radically redesigned P-47N.

Though stillborn, the attractive XP-72 nevertheless filled a small niche in aviation history as the ultimate development of the P-47.

2. P-47 in Action: Operational History

With America at war, plans centred on the defeat of Germany as an immediate priority, while Japanese military expansion was to be contained where possible. War materiel sent across the Atlantic included personnel to create the 8th Army Air Force, which would initiate a heavy bomber offensive and support an early invasion of French North Africa.

Once the 8th Bomber Command became operational, an unforeseen but increasingly urgent need arose for an effective American escort fighter in the European Theater of Operations or ETO. Britain alone could provide fighters in the ETO in the spring of 1943, and while the RAF willingly supplied many Spitfire squadrons as bomber escorts, the need for a fighter with greater range was initially met by P-47Cs and Ds. These Thunderbolts were those issued to the 56th and 78th Groups shortly after they arrived in England.

Having been the initial recipient of P-47s the 56th's pilots had had time to become thoroughly familiar with the aircraft under peacetime conditions. The 78th's experience was to train on P-38s before transferring to P-47s when its Lightnings were despatched for service in North Africa in support of Operation *Torch*. The third group slated to convert to the American fighter was the 4th, then flying Spitfires in England.

First overseas

The first P-47Cs were shipped across the Atlantic to arrive as freighter deck cargo in Liverpool or Scotland. In the UK, Republic fighters were processed through British reassembly depots operated by Lockheed Aircraft. Assembly was followed by modification, a necessary process for most US aircraft reaching overseas battlefronts to make them fit for operations. In an effort to reduce this delay Thunderbolts were first flown across the Atlantic on 25 August 1943. Ten aircraft of the 356th Group were fitted with 165-gal (137.4 Imp gal/624.6 l) P-38 tanks. One of the pilots was Barry Goldwater, who later became famous as a senator. While successful the experiment was not repeated.

The period between the German invasion of Poland and Pearl Harbor had enabled US aircraft production to pick up and some important modifications to be put in hand. Of the trio of single-engined American fighters bound for combat in the ETO/MTO in 1943, the P-47 enjoyed the greater development potential, beyond that of its immediate contemporaries, the P-39 and P-40. And although the P-47 suffered its fair share of technical drawbacks they were irritants rather than serious deficiencies. In terms of performance, the choice of a very powerful radial engine was seen to have been fortuitous, and in terms of airframe construction and firepower the Thunderbolt was in a class of its own.

Pilots continued to marvel at the sheer strength of the P-47's airframe and its potential performance, though with some reservations. It was therefore more than a little sobering to the Army Air Force, which officially announced the first P-47Cs in Britain early in 1943, to hear their RAF counterparts appearing to completely

P-47Bs of the 56th Fighter Group, circa early 1942. They are led by the CO, Hub Zemke, in aircraft No 1 (41-6002). Another future ace, Robert S Johnson, was flying No 26 (41-6011) on Zemke's wing. (*Author*)

overlook the Thunderbolt's attributes. 'Far too large and much too heavy for combat', they argued. 'Put that unwieldy monster up against a'109 or '190 and disaster for the American fighter will surely follow.' Such statements were backed by years of combat experience. The Americans had little choice but to 'bite the bullet', note the criticisms and hope their Allies were wrong. Fearing that the P-47 would be mistaken for the FW 190 in the heat of combat, recommendations were made to paint prominent white bands around the nose and vertical and horizontal tailplane. The 8th also adopted the British two-letter code system for squadron-within-group identification, a third letter denoting the individual aircraft.

Weather woes
The first AAF fighter pilots in the ETO watched in awe as British fighters took off for operational sorties in conditions that would have brought about an automatic grounding order back home. In a word, England was synonymous with weather – cold, damp, wet and cloudy weather, far too dangerous to fly in.

American pilots had no choice but to get

used to such foul conditions after the P-47C was issued to the first three 8th AAF fighter groups. The 78th was based at Goxhill in Lincolnshire, the 4th at Debden, Essex and the 56th at King's Cliffe in Northamptonshire. All underwent a period of conversion and theatre training. To help familiarise the newcomers with what they would be up against across the Channel, the RAF provided a captured Focke-Wulf FW 190. In mock combat the P-47C was found to be faster than the '190 in level flight at altitudes above 15,000 feet (4572 m); although it was unable to accelerate as well as the German fighter, it could initially keep pace with it in a turn.

In general terms, however, the Thunderbolt would lose any edge once an FW 190 pilot indulged in high-speed manoeuvres in an attempt to shake off his pursuer. But by maintaining airspeed (above 250 mph/402 km/h) for the duration of combat and using the P-47's superior diving speed the American pilot had a good chance of emerging victorious against the *Luftwaffe* single-seater.

In combat P-47s often caught up with their adversaries while in a tail chase; although

The 355th Fighter Group became operational in Europe late in 1943. Here one of the pilots poses with his P-47 in the US, just before before departing for England and the 8th Air Force.(*Author*)

nothing could touch a Thunderbolt in a high-speed dive, many *Luftwaffe* airmen appeared to forget this and continued to break and dive after making their passes on bombers. For many this was the last move they made.

Though the comparison figures were not overly encouraging for VIII Fighter Command, they were valuable in developing tactics geared to exploit the best qualities of the P-47C. The improved P-47D was about to make all this a little easier.

Increasing strength

The handful of P-47s on USAAF strength in England grew and as theatre training was completed by early April VIII Fighter Command was ready to send the first Thunderbolt sorties across the Channel.

Gradually the pilots of the 4th and 78th got the measure of their new mount, which still had a catalogue of annoying teething troubles, particularly with radio sets. If the 56th felt better placed to compensate for these problems due to its P-47 experience, it alone could not solve the technical problems stemming largely from the conditions prevailing in the new theatre of war – nor could it tempt the *Luftwaffe* into combat. The Germans bided their time, monitored the development of the American bomber offensive and devised tactics to deal with it. They soon appreciated that fully laden P-47s on bomber escort duty carried no extra fuel tanks and had to turn back miles short of Reich airspace. Staying safely beyond American fighter range the *Jagdflieger* (and the flak) began to give the American heavy bombers an ever-hotter reception.

This avoidance of combat by the *Luftwaffe* may have frustrated many an eager young fighter pilot but the 'pause' was fortunate as it

23

Drop tanks were found to be essential for P-47 escort work and some of the first were cumbersome, 200-gal belly-huggers that could only hold half that amount as they were unpressurised. A baffle was employed to break up the airflow around the tank, fitted here on an anonymous P-47C coded 'T' at Duxford. (*IWM*)

Many P-47Ds were paid for directly by the American public by war bond subscriptions. This aircraft, *Spirit of Atlantic City, New Jersey* (42-8487), was the personal mount of Capt Walker Mahurin, 63rd Fighter Squadron, 56th Group, in March 1944. (*B Robertson*)

'Orange Tails' rolling. The 358th Fighter Group was one of the 9th Air Force tactical units that used the P-47 to blast a way across Europe for the ground forces after D-Day. Visibility over the nose was minimal: the ground crewman on the wing helps guide the pilot of P-47D-10 42-75102 as he revs up for take-off. *(J Lambert)*

enabled the 8th Air Force's technical trouble shooters to concentrate on the P-47's malfunctions – which could have been highly detrimental had the pilots been embroiled in large-scale air combat immediately after they had arrived in the ETO.

Numerous short-range 'penetration' and 'withdrawal' support missions plus fighter sweeps were flown in the early summer of that year. The Americans built up their confidence in the P-47, while getting familiar with local conditions, British communications, R/T and air-sea rescue procedures. They honed their air discipline and learned most of the things they needed to know for survival in a combat zone.

Luftwaffe leaders soon appreciated the threat that the 8th Air Force's precision bombing posed to German industry. Many of the targets were airframe and engine manufacturers and while the early raids were modest in scope, the portents were alarming. By mid-1943 the German day-fighter force based in north-west Europe considered the American bombers as their primary target.

As bomber losses mounted so the call went out for more P-38 groups to be sent to the ETO to replace those siphoned off to support *Torch*. To many minds the Lightning was the only

aircraft capable of meeting a long-range escort requirement. But as P-38 groups were simply not available, a secondary answer was seen to be the fitting of suitable drop tanks to the P-47 to extend its range.

Even though such tanks existed and had been used on fighters such as the P-39 and P-40 in the US, fulfilling an overseas order was to prove challenging, time-consuming and fraught with difficulty; several makeshift tanks were tried before a teardrop-shaped 65-gal (54.1 Imp gal/246 l) belly tank could be made available in sufficient numbers. Those numbers were daunting: the current and future requirements of VIII Fighter Command ran into multiple thousands of drop tanks – enough for every fighter group then in England, not to mention those planned in the future. Tanks would be needed for every bomber escort mission flown with no foreseeable cut-off point to the supply.

Every tank had also to be assumed to be used once only, resulting in usage figures that quickly reached multiple hundreds per month, every month. It was a target that US industry could not immediately meet. A start was made, however, and when lightweight, impregnated paper tanks were also supplied from UK sources, the situation steadily improved.

Carrying a modest load of two 250-lb bombs, Lt George L Yoakum of the 361st FS, 356th Group cleans up his gear after take-off. A P-47D-20, 42-76379 has full AEAF or 'Invasion' stripes. (J Lambert)

Range gradually extended from 280 miles (450 km) to 325 miles (523 km). The *Luftwaffe*, its attention divided between US bombers and the escort, reacted and fighter clashes increased. As it transpired the 78th Group initially had the better early luck in combat. Being in the right place at the right time on some key missions, several pilots of the Duxford group scored kills over enemy fighters and began to dispel the myth that such encounters would find the P-47 wanting. Able to announce the first ETO ace by June, the 78th went from strength to strength.

On 28 July, carrying early 200-gal (166.5 Imp gal/757 l) capacity belly tanks (holding only 100 gal as they were unpressurised), P-47D-5s of the 4th Group penetrated as far as Emmerich. Totally surprising the Germans, the Debden-based unit shot down nine of them.

The 56th's luck changed in August, particularly when it met the B-17s returning from the Schweinfurt-Regensburg mission on the 17th. Up in force, the Group, known as the Wolfpack, was able to take position above the 'Big Friends' and dive onto the German fighters, cutting off many head-on passes at the heavies. The group shot down 15 enemy aircraft, claimed three probably destroyed and four damaged for the loss of three of its own.

As well as its direct contribution to defeating the *Luftwaffe*, the 56th did much to eke out the

P-47's range. By careful husbandry, its pilots were able by late 1943 to remain in the air for up to three hours, fifteen minutes. Flying Thunderbolts carrying a 108-gal (90 Imp gal/409 l) drop tank, pilots used retarded throttle and turbo settings to prevent the R-2800 from drinking precious fuel at too fast a rate. Combat often altered these carefully worked-out timings and procedures but on average the P-47D was able to remain longer in the combat zone. And every minute the fighters could stay close to the bombers counted.

Full house

As the fourth P-47 unit to be assigned to the 8th Air Force, the 353rd Group at Raydon in Suffolk went operational in August 1943 with the 352nd and 355th following suit in September. The 356th arrived in October and by December the 359th had made its operational debut. Finally, as far as the razorback P-47D was concerned, the 361st Group arrived in time to fly its first mission from Bottisham on 21 January 1944. Thus the 8th Air Force had its full complement of nine Thunderbolt groups, each with a complement recently increased to 100-108 aircraft. This was because from November 1943 it was decided that each group would henceforth fly double, 'A' and 'B' formations on each mission, thus putting the maximum

Hand-filling fuel bowsers so that aircraft could be refuelled quickly by pressure pump was the order of the day for 362nd Group ground personnel at the time of the invasion of Normandy in June 1944. This line-up of P-47D Thunderbolts of the 378th FS is headed by 42-6072, a P-47D-16. (*USAF*)

number of aircraft on escort and ground attack duty and effectively dividing the *Luftwaffe*'s response. By the turn of the year the aerial victory ratio had increased to better than three to one in the P-47's favour.

Pre-invasion build-up

In addition to its nine assigned groups of P-47Ds the 8th had, temporarily as it transpired, absorbed the 358th Fighter Group. This 9th AF unit was exchanged for the 357th which was about to join the tactical force in England flying the P-51. Revising the original plan to equip the 9th's fighter groups with Mustangs, AAF air chiefs were persuaded to channel the long-range escort fighters into the 8th while the shorter-legged P-47s became the core of the tactical 9th. Thunderbolts would therefore spearhead the air support for the forthcoming invasion of continental Europe.

By the end of 1943 the ability of the P-51 to operate at extreme range on bomber escort missions meant that some of the last Thunderbolt groups assigned to the 8th would fly the type for a few months only, as the Republic fighter would be replaced by Mustangs as soon as possible. This accelerated

Even a seven ton T-bolt could tip up and stay poised on its bent prop blades, as 358th Group pilot Jacob C Blazicek found to his cost on 17 June 1944. With a wing badly chewed up by flak on a mission over the front, P-47D-20 42-76436 of the 367th FS was lucky to make it back to a forward strip – but then P-47s were doing that almost daily in June 1944! (*IWM*)

A censored serial number cannot detract much from this P-47D (2Z-P) of the 405th Group, as it strikes a pugnacious pose in full D-Day paint and large wing insignia. The pilot was Bruce Parcell, CO of the 510th Squadron, who was killed later in 1944 while strafing a train in France. (*J V Crow*)

replacement programme meant that other than the 56th, only the 78th, 353rd and 356th Groups received any bubbletop models before P-51Bs came along.

The advent of the P-51 released more Thunderbolts as replacements for the units on tactical operations and no less than 14 of the 18 groups of the 9th were equipped with the P-47D by the spring of 1944. In materiel terms this meant that by May there were about 1,800 P-47s in two US air forces available for operations from England.

On arrival in England personnel of the 9th Air Force's P-47 groups had confirmation that their main duty would be ground attack, a role tailor-made for an air-cooled radial-engined fighter. The P-47 was statistically less vulnerable to ground fire than the P-51, which could be disabled by a loss of engine coolant.

In July 1943 8th Air Force P-47 units had begun paving the way in ground strafing. Pilots returning from escort missions with enough ammunition would drop down and shoot up any worthwhile target. By early 1944 enough 8th Air Force P-47s were available to indirectly support the bombers by attacking enemy airfields, transport, troop concentrations and other targets under the air routes into Germany. More elaborately planned 8th AAF fighter bomber operations had followed and the newcomer 9th AAF groups benefited from this accumulated data. Basing much of their tactical doctrine on what both the 8th and 12th Air Forces had already achieved, these groups also flew bomber escort missions for a little variety. Few pilots, offered the chance to have a crack at the *Luftwaffe*, disagreed with that policy.

Multi-Role

All types of target were to present themselves to American pilots flying P-47s in the ETO – where the Republic fighter became a true 'master of all work' – and they fulfilled several exacting roles including those of anti-tank and dive bomber. Despite the latter role figuring strongly in pre-war USAAC planning, the Army lost enthusiasm and never did field a successful dive bomber after the A-36. The P-47 filled the gap admirably.

Similar good results were obtained on tank-

This famous view of a P-47D-22 of the 410th FS, 373rd Group was taken over the Abbey of Mont St Michel off the coast of Brittany. The occasion was a press facility for photographer Charles E Brown who was visiting the unit. Brown took this picture from a Piper Cub flown by the group CO, William H Schwartz. (*USAF*)

busting sorties and although the P-47 was never directly classified as an anti-armour aircraft because it carried no specialised weapons such as heavy cannon, there were numerous occasions when 9th AAF Thunderbolts destroyed and crippled AFVs using guns, bombs and rockets. Pioneering ground attacks by the 8th Air Force's P-47 groups had determined the optimum dive angle, the right speed during target approach, the composition and direction of the various elements, and the most effective ordnance to use. As a fighter, dive bomber and anti-tank aircraft the P-47 exemplified the generic term 'fighter bomber' which merged all these overlapping roles.

In north-west Europe, 1944 began positively for the Allies. With hundreds of its P-47 pilots having scored one or more aerial victories, the 8th Air Force anticipated forthcoming bomber support operations with much more confidence than had been the case the year before. Equally, the Thunderbolt groups of the 9th AAF were building up invaluable experience on numerous sorties across the Channel, softening up the enemy defences prior to the invasion. On 24 January AAF chiefs confirmed that most of the 8th's fighter groups would be re-equipped with Mustangs, the P-47s and P-38s being transferred over a period of time.

Big Week

By 20 February enough 150-gal (125 Imp gal/568 l) belly tanks were available for VIII Fighter Command's P-47 groups to carry them into the intensive round of missions known as Big Week (20–25 February). The tanks allowed 15 minutes' more flying time, giving the P-47D the ability to operate 350 miles (563 km) from home base. This period was marked by a victory total of 218 enemy aircraft shot down, the majority by Thunderbolt pilots. On 22 February the Wolfpack's 61st Squadron celebrated its prowess with the P-47 by claiming its 100th victory in aerial combat. In March the 56th extended its radius of action by carrying two

Seen in June 1944, soon after the Normandy invasion, this P-47D-27 (D3-Z/42-26937) of the 397th FS, 368th Group, is bombed up and ready to launch at a moment's notice from airfield A-3 Cardonville, France. Again, note the additional oversize underwing insignia added for recognition purposes. *(J Lambert)*

108-gal (90 Imp gal/409 l) drop tanks; this meant that for the first time the P-47s could remain in the air for over four hours. Pilots had to keep a watchful eye on their fuel gauges for although drop tanks could take them deep into German-occupied territory, once that fuel was used up, they had about an hour and a half of flying time before the internal tanks ran dry. The timely delivery of the first P-47D-25s to UK-based groups in May enabled a further boost in range by virtue of the extra 65 gal (54.1 Imp gal/246 l) of fuel carried internally by the first bubbletop Thunderbolt model.

Following the Torch

P-47s generally replaced P-40s, P-39s and A-36s flown by US fighter groups in the Mediterranean during the first six months of 1944. The AAF had re-established the old 9th Air Force in England, retained the tactical 12th in the MTO, and created the 15th Air Force in Italy. One of the transferees to the new air force was the 325th Group, the famed Checkertails. The unit began receiving razorback P-47D models in November 1943 primarily for the

bomber escort role which it was to share with three groups of P-38s.

Between January and June 1944 the 12th's tactical groups – the 57th, 79th and 27th (in that order) – had all re-equipped with P-47s, bringing about a major increase in firepower and performance appreciated by all concerned.

By the time of the Allied amphibious landing at Anzio, ostensibly to speed the capture of Rome, USAAF and RAF airpower in the area was comfortably strong. Axis reaction to the invasion was vigorous, however, and a substantial force of *Luftwaffe* bombers and dive bombers was concentrated on a number of airfields in northern Italy. As these enemy units represented a potential danger to Allied operations at Anzio, the 325th Group carried out a surprise two-pronged attack on 30 January 1944. While the Thunderbolts dive-bombed and strafed, a force of 15th Air Force heavies plastered the area. All went according to plan; the 325th claimed about 60 enemy aircraft destroyed and the simultaneous bomber missions knocked out further aircraft and wrecked ground installations.

Still largely intact after a forced landing, P-47D *Nancy* of the 511th Squadron, 405th Group is inspected by passing GIs during a lull in fighting on their sector of the front. (*IWM*)

The 325th then flew 'plain' Thunderbolts without the striking yellow and black 'checkertail' markings which were applied later. The group alone provided single-engine fighter escort to the 15th's heavies before enough P-51s were available from May 1944 to replace the Thunderbolts.

Tuskegee Airmen

One unit that rose to prominence mainly after its brief (April to June 1944) P-47 period was the all-black 322nd Fighter Group. Destined for escort work with P-51s, the group relinquished P-40s and kept its hand in by flying hand-me-down P-47s, several of them from the 325th and 57th Groups. The 322nd's famous 'red tails' first began to appear on the Thunderbolts.

Attacking targets on the ground remained the daily fare of the P-47 groups in all war theatres and for the 12th Air Force groups in particular. With the progressive re-equipment of the 86th, 324th and 350th Fighter Groups with razorback and bubbletop P-47s by mid-1944, the MTO fighter bomber force continued the interdiction of transport links begun under Operation *Strangle*, hitting the German supply lines above Rome and gradually squeezing the Axis into a northern Italian enclave.

Joining the American Thunderbolt groups in the theatre in October was 1⁰ *Grupo de Aviacao*

de Caca of the Brazilian Air Force. The unit flew its first P-47 mission on 31 October. Wartime allocation to the *Forca Aerea Brasileira* for its Mediterranean deployment totalled 88 P-47s, all bubbletop models. Unit establishment was 25 aircraft, and at the end of hostilities the Brazilians returned home from Pisa with a total of 26 P-47s remaining from wartime inventory.

Last but by no means least, the MTO saw the re-equipped *Armée de l'Air* operating as the 1st French Air Corps, part of the US 1st Tactical Air Force. It raised six P-47 units, the first of three *Groupes de Chasse* being activated on Corsica. Co-located on Alto airfield with the 57th Fighter Group, *Groupe de Chasse* II/3 *Dauphine* began flying P-47 ground attack sorties on 1 May 1944.

Five further *Groupes de Chasse* – III/3 *Ardennes*, I/4 *Navarre*, I/5 *Champagne*, II/5 *La Fayette* and III/6 *Roussillon* – flew P-47s, the last named starting to fly combat missions in bubbletop D models on 1 February 1945.

Invasion support

With D-Day a reality American P-47, P-38 and P-51 fighter bombers wrought terrible destruction on enemy ground forces that threatened the Allied beachhead. Assigned to IX, XIX and XXIX Tactical Air Commands, each supporting a separate US army, the P-47 groups

A P-47D-22 (42-26272) of the 361st FS, 356th Group slides in to take a closer look at a 458th Bomb Group B-24 Liberator. *Angel Eyes* was flown by Capt Howard E Wiggins. (*via M Bowman*)

would experience a considerable switching of higher command as the war in north-west Europe progressed. This mattered little as the work they did was generally similar – only the degree of danger they faced (increasingly from German flak rather than the *Luftwaffe*) varied. Relying heavily on mobile batteries of quad 20-mm AA guns, the Germans could put up veritable curtains of explosive ammunition and being highly skilled at camouflaging equipment, they often sprang traps for fighter bombers by lacing small areas of sky with fire.

Into Europe

Leaving England to occupy continental airfields as soon as these could be made ready, the 9th's P-47 groups ably assisted the Allied ground forces at very reduced flying ranges. The process had begun with the 358th Group, on 16 July. In France 9th Air Force service echelons had often to overcome unbelievably primitive conditions to 'keep 'em flying.'

At some locations a good servicing area meant a hangar with part of the roof still intact after Allied bombing had passed that way.

Tents came into their own on devastated ex-*Luftwaffe* aerodromes, which were more often than not wrecked by the retreating Germans if Allied air power had not already done the job. Living and servicing aeroplanes under canvas was one thing in summer – in the bitter depths of winter such as that which hit Europe in 1944-45, it was close to purgatory. And needless to say the kind of tactical war the P-47 groups were fighting was not won without casualties. Badly damaged aircraft that made it back to Allied lines were repaired *in situ* if possible, while those beyond economical repair were cannibalised for parts to keep others flying. Fortunately Air Service Command had established a massive supply depot at Burtonwood in Lancashire which ferried new and repaired aircraft to the combat groups whenever they were needed.

That flak claimed the majority of P-47s lost in Europe during 1944-45 was starkly emphasised for the 56th Group during September 1944. Beginning the month on a high note, VIII FC sent four P-47 groups out on strafing missions. Pilots of 138 aircraft shot up 94 locomotives,

A typical mix of P-47 models shown in a two-ship section of the 361st FS, 356th Group. Nearest is Capt Edward L Faison's P-47D-28, 42-228827/QI-I, with razorback D-15 42-76277/QI-P on his wing. Note that the wing leading edge of the bubbletop has been cleaned back to natural metal finish to improve performance. (*Author*)

Flying out of Duxford until December 1944, when it re-equipped with P-51s, the 78th Group was one of the longest-serving Thunderbolt units in the 8th Air Force. This well-photographed P-47D-25, 42-26635 was flown by Capt Richard A Hewitt for a series of publicity shots. (*P Jarrett*)

Flying low over the sea, probably the Adriatic, a bubbletop P-47D with the striking red and white tail stripes of the 86th Fighter Group and the number '45' to denote an aircraft of the 526th FS, heads out for (or home from) a mission during the Italian campaign. (*Lambert*)

damaged 20 more and claimed also to have destroyed 537 items of rolling stock and 382 vehicles. On the 5th the Thunderbolts went after *Luftwaffe* airfields, the 56th Fighter Group claiming 60 aircraft destroyed on the ground for the loss of six P-47s.

Such success was typical, but it had to be offset later that month with an ill-fated operation not of the Wolfpack's making. Supporting Operation *Market Garden*, the attempt to cross the Rhine at Arnhem, brought about the group's blackest period. On the 17th the 56th's P-47s, in company with those of the 78th, 353rd and 356th Groups, put up 200 aircraft to attack enemy flak in the Arnhem area, with a similar operation taking place the following day. German ground fire was vicious and out of 39 Wolfpack P-47s participating, 16 were posted as missing. Other losses during September brought the 8th's debit table to 73

fighters, 45 of them P-47s. The Wolfpack's total of 18 losses on Arnhem support missions were the highest of the war.

Attack in the Ardennes

By the autumn of 1944 preparations were being made to cross the Rhine once the weather improved. As Christmas approached, winter intervened with a vengeance, giving the Germans a slim chance of reversing a disastrous military position. On 16 December they struck. Breaking through thinly held lines in the Ardennes Forest region, ten Panzer divisions gained ground under cover of fog, snow and rain that prevented tactical air forces from detecting any sign of a major counter-offensive. For a few vital days the Allies were obliged to retreat. Only when the skies cleared on 23 December did a rain of fire from the air begin to blunt the advance. Once the enemy

A P-47D-25 (42-26448) of the 65th Squadron, 57th Group on Corsica in 1944. The group and the island were featured in William Wyler's fine wartime documentary film, 'Thunderbolt'. (*Crow*)

began losing irreplaceable tanks and other vehicles to air attack the outcome of the Battle of the Bulge was never in doubt.

As always, tactical P-47 groups had to make due allowance for the weather. The view was that the elements were definitely siding with the Germans during the winter of 1944–45, snow and fog giving the American fighter bombers difficulties in locating objectives, particularly under the canopy of dense forests.

During the later stages of the Ardennes battle 9th AAF fighters used guns, bombs and rockets to steadily whittle down the strength the enemy had so carefully marshalled for this daring but desperate gamble. Numerous hazardous P-47 sorties were flown against AFVs and soft-skinned vehicles, for the German road convoys invariably included their own mobile flak. Losses in some groups were consequently quite heavy but once air and ground forces could coordinate again, obstacles that threatened Allied forces were systematically eliminated. Such good ground-to-air liaison was established that army commanders enjoyed the continual reassurance that air cover was only minutes away. And an attack by a P-47 outfit could usually be relied upon to clear the way, even if the enemy had been giving the GIs a

hard time before their air cover arrived.

Occasionally fighting off the *Luftwaffe* in order to carry out their ground attack missions, the 9th's Thunderbolt flyers took on and invariably beat all comers. Even the feared Me 262 jet could do little to prevent them providing their brilliantly executed, relentless support service.

Luftwaffe's last throw

Then on 1 January 1945 a last throw by the *Luftwaffe* known as Operation *Bodenplatte* caught some tactical squadrons on the ground. Of the 9th Air Force P-47 units based in Belgium, the worst hit was the 365th Group at Metz. Most of a single squadron's complement of Thunderbolts succumbed to strafing and for some time it was forced to borrow other aircraft to meet mission schedules.

During *Bodenplatte* there was an incident that resulted in what was claimed to be the first-ever air-to-air destruction of a fighter by a missile, in this case an M-10 'Bazooka' rocket. Sighting quickly as the German attack developed, Mel Paisley of the 366th Group fired a salvo to bring down a Bf 109 in the vicinity of his base at Asche.

As a result of the policy of re-equipping the

35

Billie was a P-47D-28 of the 66th FS, which as part of the 57th Group carried its large fighting cock badge on an equally large and distinctive white cross on the cowling of its Thunderbolts. (*McDowell*)

As the war in Europe wound down, the colour schemes of 9th Air Force P-47Ds tended to grow more flamboyant as *Mil O Mine* of the 368th Group shows. The flash was dark blue, denoting the 397th FS. (*J Campbell*)

Die Luftwaffe ist kaput – a peaceful field at Straubing, Germany in 1945 symbolises Germany's defeat as P-47Ds of the 405th Group park alongside their erstwhile antagonists, three Fw 190F-8s. (*Crow*)

entire 8th Fighter Command with the P-51, Thunderbolt units had become rare in England by early 1945. The previous December the 78th at Duxford had made the transition, leaving just the 56th, the 'original' P-47 outfit. News that their beloved T-bolts might soon be replaced by 'Span cans' (Mustangs) spread gloom amongst pilots and groundcrew, and requests were made to stave this off. Officialdom relented. In the light of its outstanding combat record the 56th Fighter Group was allowed to retain P-47s and an entirely new model was to be shipped to England for exclusive use by the Wolfpack. This was the P-47M, which promised to be an outstanding combat aircraft.

Unfortunately the Wolfpack's eager-beaver pilots were initially denied a chance to exploit the qualities of the P-47M due to engine problems. For the time being, the 56th reverted to the P-47D to maintain its mission schedules. The new aircraft was 'back on the line' in January 1945 and as the war in Europe still had a few months to run, the Wolfpack was able to exploit the potential of the M model on numerous occasions, examples being flown by all the group's late-war aces.

In Germany, major Allied air offensives such as Operation *Clarion* denied the *Wehrmacht* the last remnants of a cohesive transport and supply system. P-47 groups strafed trains, bombed marshalling yards, shot up river barges and 'defended buildings', in the process so totally interdicting the roads that German travel in daylight was little short of suicidal.

Ultimately the AAF tactical squadrons simply ran out of targets. As the Allied armies tightened the noose, there was little left for them to shoot at. Now pilots had to check their coordinates particularly carefully lest the troops below them were friendly, for the advance into some areas where German resistance was weak proceeded very swiftly. By the spring the ETO combat groups were gradually stood down.

Mass strafing

On 13 April 1945 the 56th carried out its most successful strafing attack of the war. For several days previously the brightly painted P-47Ms had gone out and found targets – but these were rapidly diminishing in terms of value to a defeated enemy. Finding Eggebeck aerodrome full of enemy aircraft, the pilots of 50 Thunderbolts went on a shooting spree, returning to England with a tally of 95 destroyed. True to its deadly reputation, enemy flak nailed the P-47M-1 (44-21134) flown by Lt William Hoffman, who was the last pilot of the group to be killed in action.

On 21 April the Wolfpack flew its last

The 1st Air Commando Group originally applied white diagonal fuselage stripes on its camouflaged P-51s. The replacement Thunderbolts, including razorbacks and P-47D-30s, were in NMF so the fuselage stripes were painted in dark blue. The nose, wings and tail also carried bands in line with SEAC recommendations. (*Jarrett*)

mission of the war. Its final tally was 677 enemy aircraft destroyed in aerial combat for the loss of 128 P-47s, a kill ratio better than five to one.

With the German surrender on 8 May several USAAF Thunderbolt groups designated for German occupation duty settled into their new homes. All 9th Air Force units had been operating from German soil since mid-March 1945 and these now flew their last missions from the 'enemy's own backyard', as some pilots might have put it with a degree of ill-disguised satisfaction.

Asia and the Pacific

P-47s reached the China-Burma-India theatre in April 1944 when the 10th and 14th Air Forces shared the 33rd Fighter Group. With personnel having arrived in India from the Mediterranean, the unit's P-47s were ferried to Karachi aboard two carriers. While the group's 58th and 60th Squadrons completed transition training on the Thunderbolt the 59th FS equipped with P-40Ns. Selected by the 312th Fighter Wing to protect forward B-29 bases in China under the *Matterhorn* plan, the 33rd moved to the southern central region of that country on 5 June to occupy three airfields around the provincial capital, Chengdu. The group's first P-47 mission took place on 29 April.

The group also flew a number of sorties to escort B-29 night raids when these went out in the afternoon; in the morning they shepherded the Superforts in on their return to China. But due to the fact that the B-29 bases were within range of enemy aircraft the *Matterhorn* experiment was abandoned and the Superfortresses moved out to conduct their offensive from the Marianas. In September the 33rd, back under the direct command of the 10th Air Force, returned to India. From airfields in the Assam valley the 33rd and 80th Groups (which went operational with P-47s in May) used their P-47s to good effect in the ground attack role, supporting Stilwell's actions against the Japanese in Burma. Sorties were often co-ordinated with those of RAF Thunderbolt squadrons.

The 81st Fighter Group also arrived in China, on 12 May. Another transferee from the MTO, the group flew its first P-47D mission on 1 June. It would remain as part of the 14th Air Force and after a break on training duties, returned to combat before the end of the war. During this period the 81st's pilots scored four victories. A 'first' for the P-47 in China was a Ki-46 shot down on 4 July.

Containing the Japanese in Burma proved marginally easier than in China, where not only did large tracts of land remain in enemy hands but all Allied supplies had to be flown in over the Hump. That included fuel for fighters and the heavy consumption of the P-47 did not exactly endear it to theatre commanders. That

Thunder over the islands. A squadron of P-47Ns from the yellow-tailed 507th FG cross the coast, probably of their island base of Ie Shima, during 1945. *(Lambert)*

was the major reason why the P-40 and P-51 predominated in that area. Japanese offensives in China continued until much later in the war than anywhere else and the threat to Allied air bases resulted in a degree of shuttling back and forth of AAF fighter groups, either in their entirety or as individual squadrons.

As well as American-manned P-47s, a substantial number of Lend-Lease razorback and bubbletop P-47Ds arrived in China throughout 1944–45. Chinese pilots saw little if any air combat with the Japanese whilst flying P-47s during hostilities but many aircraft, their

numbers boosted by ex-American machines left behind at the end of the war, served the Nationalist cause during the years of postwar upheaval.

Also flying P-47s over Burma was the 1st Air Commando Group which operated two squadrons of P-47s, the 5th and 6th, from September 1944. This experimental unit more than proved its worth in support of small scale, mobile and virtually self-supporting commando operations similar to those conceived by Orde Wingate for his Chindits. The air element also operated as a self-

Having destroyed nine German aircraft in Europe flying Mustangs with the 361st Group, including two Me 262s in a single mission, Urban Drew took a tour in the Pacific with the 7th Air Force. Seen here in a P-47N-5 of the 413th FS, 414th Group, he felt great respect for the Thunderbolt but on balance preferred the P-51. (*Drew*)

contained unit as far as possible and 1st Air Commando Group Thunderbolts, both razorback and bubbletop models, were used until replaced by Mustangs in May 1945.

Pacific debut in New Guinea

Range also became of paramount importance to the 348th Fighter Group, which arrived in Australia to fly the first P-47Ds in the Pacific during August 1943. Destined to take the war to the Japanese from forward bases in New Guinea, the unit quickly came to terms with facilities that were primitive at best. Drip-fed supplies at the end of a very long line, George Kenney's 5th Air Force approached suppliers in Australia for the drop tanks the 348th needed. Several makeshift installations holding up to 200 US gallons (166.5 Imp gal/757 l) were also made by Air Service Command in Port Moresby before a suitable 108 gal (90 Imp gal/408.8 l) belly tank became available.

In a theatre where the P-38 was king, the P-47's Pacific war service extended to operations with three full groups. The 348th was joined by the 35th and 58th Groups which made their Pacific combat debuts in New Guinea in

December 1943 and February 1944 respectively. In addition the 8th Group converted its 36th Squadron and the 49th its 35th Squadron to P-47s, mainly as a result of shortages of P-38s.

Distance had a significant bearing on shortages suffered by the 5th Air Force as seaborne equipment had to traverse much of the Pacific before reaching squadrons in the SWPA. In the case of the P-47 only 207 examples had reached Australia by December 1943 and these needed processing and checking before undertaking the 1,200 mile (1930 km) staged flight to Port Moresby and the forward operating airfields.

To the surprise of some sceptics, the Thunderbolt did well in the 'war of the islands' which enjoyed a very hostile climate as well as primitive facilities. Up against agile but lightly armoured Japanese fighters, particularly the Army Ki-43 Oscar, Ki-61 Tony and Navy A6M Zeke, the P-47D generally gave a good account of itself. Provided that they could avoid being drawn into dogfighting below 16,000 ft (4877 m) and could employ the 'dive and zoom climb' tactics used sucessfully by P-39s and P-40s, American pilots made good use of their

With a striking ace of spades and death's head badge on its Thunderbolts, No 73 OTU at Fayid, Egypt was the first RAF unit to fly the Republic fighter extensively. Mk I HD176 is pictured here. (*Author*)

superior firepower, often with devastating results. Japanese Army and Navy fighters and bombers had a propensity to burn easily and by late 1943 combat attrition had definitely reduced pilot quality.

On 26 December 1943 the 8th Fighter Group gave outstanding support to the invasion of New Britain. P-47s of the 36th Squadron, in company with the 35th's P-40s and P-38s of the 431st, intercepted a 75-strong Japanese air element bent on disrupting the operation at Cape Gloucester. The mixed US force attacked and was later joined by two Thunderbolt squadrons from the 348th Group. In total P-47s were credited with shooting down 15 enemy bombers and two fighters. By year's end the latter group's 342nd FS had claimed a total of 79 enemy aircraft destroyed.

Battle in the Marianas

Following an April 1944 decision by the US to invade the Mariana Islands and thus secure bases for the B-29 force, the 318th Group of the 7th Air Force embarked its P-47Ds on two escort carriers that June. Catapulted off the carriers, the T-bolts headed for Aslito Field on Saipan where they were quickly made ready to mount strikes on neighbouring Tinian.

Ably assisting American ground forces in capturing all three main islands in the Marianas chain, two squadrons of the 318th began operations from Saipan while Japanese troops were still fighting on the island. The enemy surrendered on 9 July and by the 17th the 318th's P-47s had completed 2,500 sorties.

The following day the group's third squadron arrived to continue mopping-up operations and extend its reach with sorties out to Iwo Jima, the unit's razorback P-47Ds often acting as escort to B-24s. During this period group aircraft also dropped napalm bombs for the first time.

By February 1944 the 8th Fighter Group's P-47s had been replaced by P-38s, much to the relief of many pilots. That was not a universal view, some pilots having appreciated the P-47's qualities without unfavourable comparisons. But to fighter pilots used to the safety factor of two engines, flying a single-engined aircraft over vast, largely impenetrable jungle and miles of ocean undeniably carried a great deal more risk. Not that the P-47 was found wanting: General Ennis Whitehead of V Fighter Command was fullsome in his praise, at one time calling the Thunderbolt 'the best fighter our country possesses'.

41

In action the Thunderbolt Mk I soon endeared itself to the RAF pilots pounding the Japanese army in Burma. Most sorties involved bombing and strafing enemy troops and jungle supply routes. (*via A Thomas*)

Return to the Philippines

By August 1944 Douglas MacArthur prepared to lead a massive amphibious assault to retake the Philippines. As part of the 5th Air Force's support for the invasion of Leyte the 348th Group acquired a fourth squadron. Flying new P-47D-23s, the presence of the 460th Squadron made its parent group the only one of its size in the SWPA. Over 400 P-47s were available for the invasion and early indirect operations in support of MacArthur's venture began for the 35th Group based on Morotai with strafing enemy airfields on Negros.

The group hit the Balikpapan oil fields in Borneo between 8 and 10 October, by which time the 40th and 41st Squadrons were flying P-47D-28s adapted to take the 35th Group's own long-range fuel combination. In order for their pilots to reach a target that lay 835 miles from their base, the engineers had rigged a 310-gal (258 Imp gal/1173 l) tank on one wing with a 165-gal (141.8 Imp gal/624.5 l) tank on the other. A 75-gal (64.5 Imp gal/284 l) tank under the belly was retained throughout the mission. Although this fuel combination got the group to Balikpapan, there was little reserve for combat. Nevertheless, by diving from high altitude, the unit's pilots shot down 15 enemy aircraft during the course of these missions. Two US pilots were lost.

By 10 November following the successful invasion, the 348th Fighter Group's 460th FS had moved up to Leyte. There the P-47s joined with other Allied aircraft for an intensive round of air strikes against Japanese positions.

December saw P-47 attacks on Palompon and Leyte and missions to escort bombers pounding the Japanese occupants of Clark Field. On 17 December the 460th's P-47s were the first US fighters to appear over the Philippine capital Manila. During that month the enemy made a determined attempt to wreck the US invasion, and FEAF fighters became involved in desperate attempts to turn IJN ships away from vulnerable transports supporting the beachhead.

In a series of combats ten P-47s were lost but the transports were saved. During the invasion of Luzon which began in January 1945, P-47s undertook an increasing number of ground strafing missions. On 16 May, P-47s formed part of a 673-strong fighter bomber force sent out to support a battle raging at Ipo on Luzon. Six square miles of Japanese held territory were strafed and deluged with napalm, totally overwhelming the defenders.

A line-up of Thunderbolt Mk IIs of No 81 Squadron, possibly in Java. Many RAF machines retained their full camouflage and white SEAC bands until the war's end and beyond. (*via A Thomas*)

By March 1945, with the older P-47Ds being replaced by Mustangs in 5th Air Force groups, a second build-up of Thunderbolts took place with 451 aircraft, mostly P-47Ns, arriving in the central Pacific area. Four groups of the 7th Air Force, the 318th, 413th, 414th and 507th, had been equipped with the last Thunderbolt model to be delivered in time to see combat.

P-47s over Japan

In May the 318th Group flew its debut missions in the P-47N and on the 25th the group was ranging over Kyushu. By destroying 34 enemy aircraft, including would-be kamikazes, the Army pilots undoubtedly saved the lives of some of their naval colleagues in the US fleet. The month also saw the start of night harassment missions by P-47Ns when two aircraft from Okinawa initiated a series of strikes that lasted until 10 June. Hazardous and in the opinion of the pilots hardly necessary, this experiment was taken over by P-61s which were better suited to nocturnal operations.

Arriving in time to participate in the latter stages of the Philippines operation were ex-58th Group P-47Ds passed to 201 *Escuadron, Fuerza Aerea Mexicana*, which completed a single combat tour. Attached to the 58th Fighter Group from 7 June to 9 August 1945, the Mexican Expeditionary Air Force used a total of 22 early-model Thunderbolts and flew 42 ground attack missions before 25 P-47D-30s were assigned in June 1945.

By the end of June the rampaging 318th Group had brought its total of enemy aircraft destroyed to 108. This hectic period saw some desperate last-ditch actions on the part of the Japanese, making a last-gasp attempt to whittle down Allied fighter strength on several bases including Ie Shima. On the 13th, the Thunderbolts downed 48 for the loss of three of their own, a total of 244 enemy aircraft sorties being noted. A kamikaze attack on the US fleet on 22 June was intercepted by P-47Ns of the 413th Group, pilots claiming seven of the would-be suicide aircraft.

Now operating regularly over the Japanese home islands, the 7th AAF P-47s helped to neutralise airfields, military installations and harbour facilities in preparation for the Allied invasion planned for the end of that year or in 1946. The AAF also began sending Thunderbolts to escort bombers attacking Japan. On 5 July, 102 aircraft shepherded B-25s and B-24s which blasted targets in Kyushu.

Ground attack

On 5 August the 5th and 7th Air Forces combined their stength to mount a massive assault on Tarumizu, where rocket-propelled kamikaze aircraft were manufactured. Heavy and medium bombers plus fighters carried out the strike which included 97 P-47s attacking the target with GP bombs and napalm. Three days later the 301st Fighter Wing, comprising elements of the entire P-47N force, escorted 400 B-29s to Yawata. That city was the next on the USAAF target list after Hiroshima, which had been devastated by an atomic bomb two days previously.

The Japanese sent up 60 fighters to intercept the Superfortresses, and the Thunderbolts waded in to claim 13 shot down for four of their own. This was the only occasion that the

A Thunderbolt Mk II of No 134 Squadron runs up its engine soon after the surrender of Japan. No. 134 was one of the units which operated NMF Thunderbolts with dark blue SEAC recognition markings. (*L Manwaring*)

301st FW mounted a B-29 escort, such duty having by that stage of war been largely taken over by P-51s. However, some B-29 raids were not escorted at all, as Japan's air defence was generally weak. On 11 August P-47Ns of the 318th Group bombed a damaged rail bridge on the east coast of Kyushu and successfully finished off a job begun earlier by bombers.

Long-range P-47N sorties also took in Japanese training bases in Korea, where several pilots were able to score the war's last victories over enemy aircraft in that area. On 13 August the 507th Group clashed with 50 Japanese aircraft. Resulting combats saw two P-47Ns downed for 20 of the enemy. Two days later Japan surrendered to bring WWII to a close.

RAF Thunderbolts

Even before the establishment of No 73 Operational Training Unit as the Thunderbolt OTU at Fayid, Egypt in 1944, the RAF's association with the type had been quite extensive. Long before a single P-47 ever fired a shot in anger, in an entirely different theatre of war, the A & AEE at Boscombe Down had tested aircraft borrowed from the USAAF, as well as several allocated directly to the British.

Burma was the war theatre selected for the deployment of Thunderbolts by the RAF. By the spring of 1944 South-East Asia Command (SEAC) was keen to replace ageing Hurricanes

in a number of squadrons which were attacking the deprived and demoralised but still-dangerous Japanese Army.

Nos 5, 30, 79, 123, 134, 135, 146, 258 and 261 Squadrons became operational with P-47s during 1944, with Nos 34, 42, 60, 81, 113, 131 and 615 following suit in 1945. Of these, Nos 134 and 135 were first to go into combat in May 1944. Both units, in common with others activated that year, flew a mix of Thunderbolt Mks I and II. The bubbletop Mk II predominated in 1945, although the razorback Mk I was around until the end of the war.

Although they rarely met the enemy in aerial combat, the pilots of the SEAC Thunderbolt squadrons developed a loyalty and respect equal to that of their US counterparts for one of the world's finest fighter bombers. Harrying the Japanese Army as it retreated out of Burma, these units carried out numerous strafing and dive bombing attacks. The technique for the latter had to be modified to adopt a shallower approach; if a near-vertical angle was used pull-out could be too marginal for safety.

Few of the pilots involved failed to be impressed at the way the Thunderbolt's eight guns were able to rip apart the flimsy native bashas that offered scant protection for Japanese radio stations, troops and vehicles. River traffic, mostly small vessels and barges, proved equally easy meat for the rampaging

With the war in Europe over, the 56th Fighter Group turned in its P-47Ds and Ms and returned to the USA, reforming on P-47Ns in 1946. The group had flown the P-47 for longer than any other unit, with experience on every variant. This P-47N-5 (44-88680) bears the bright red nose and tail markings in vogue at that time. (*MAP*)

Thunderbolts. Monsoon weather was occasionally more of a hazard than the enemy; torrential rain could easily wash away forward airstrips and lead to temporary groundings. But throughout the later stages of the Burma campaign RAF Thunderbolts ably supported General William Slim's 14th Army in its drive to liberate the country.

P-47s on the Eastern Front

Thunderbolts also appeared in combat on the Eastern Front, where the Red Air Force had absorbed American Lend-Lease supplies of aircraft. The 195 P-47Ds included razorback D-10s and D-22s and bubbletop D-27s. Only three aircraft were flown direct over the Alaska-Siberia supply route, the balance being sent by sea via the South Atlantic where seven were lost prior to delivery.

At least four combat units flew the P-47 in VVS (Soviet Air Force) service although the number despatched was miniscule compared to other US fighters. Some 9,200 aircraft were delivered to Russia, the bulk being provided by such types as the P-39, P-63 and the P-40.

With little peacetime requirement for the P-47 (soon to be redesignated the F-47) by the new United States Air Force, reduction of the type in all former theatres of war was quite rapid, although few other areas had as many groups as did the 9th and 12th Air Forces in Europe. In the Pacific combat group personnel went home, abandoning their aircraft on the last airfields their units had reached during the advance on Japan. The cost of transporting what now amounted to so much scrap metal was not even contemplated by officialdom. Many were smelted down *in situ*.

Preferring not to round off its fine 8th Air Force record without a last flourish of publicity, the 56th painted some of its combat statistics on a P-47M (44-21175) and sent it to Paris for public exhibition under the Eiffel Tower as part of an Allied air forces victory display.

Overtaken by Jets

By autumn 1945 obsolescence had already overtaken warplanes rated among the world's best some two months previously. In the US the first turbojet fighters relegated the P-47 and its contemporaries to second-line status quite rapidly. However, there was still some life ahead of the P-47. France, Brazil and Mexico welcomed the gift of US aircraft to build the foundations of their respective postwar air arms. France had had her industry shattered in 1940 and the country operated dozens of Allied

No less than 28 Air National Guard squadrons flew the P-47D and N, early postwar markings being quite low-key. This Massachusetts NG line-up of Thunderbolts has a P-47N-20 (44-89123) nearest the camera with non-standard size serial and branch-of-service abbreviation on the fin. (*H Holmes*)

and Axis aircraft types until indigenous production could begin again. In Latin America, the P-47 was regarded as a modern enough type from 1945 into the 1950s.

Home front

In total the P-47 had fully or partially equipped no less than 66 wartime fighter, reconnaissance, commando and replacement training groups across the US and around the world. The training of replacement pilots had accelerated in 1942. By mid-1944 some of the RTUs were closed, the supply of pilots intended for the combat theatres being more or less fulfilled by that time.

At home and abroad several of the old AAF units, including the 14th, 23rd and 79th Fighter Groups, continued to fly the P(F)-47. Several aircraft of the latter unit even retained their striking blue with gold lightning flash tail marking along with the USAF's modified national insignia with red bars added. The 56th Fighter Group was reactivated in May 1945 and issued with P-47Ns and Mustangs.

On Guam the 23rd Fighter Group, having relinquished its P-51s, became a Thunderbolt outfit, as did the 21st FG, another wartime Mustang unit. The 51st Group was reactivated in 1946 and operated out of Okinawa with F-47s and F-61s until 1948.

Postwar activities by USAAF/USAF P-47s were concentrated in Europe under the umbrella of the 86th Fighter/Fighter Bomber Group which became something of a 'holding unit'. Once the regular occupation troops had rotated home and many of their aircraft and units had been dispersed, the 86th remained to represent a modest bastion in early Cold War days, its pilots and aircraft helping to maintain a ready alert in the event that Soviet sabre rattling turned into something more aggressive pending the arrival of the first operational USAF jet fighter units.

A little light relief was provided when in 1950 the 86th furnished a squadron of F-47Ds to act as a Russian fighter unit for a feature film on the Berlin airlift. Complete with liberally applied red stars and false canopy bars to denote Lavochkins or whatever the producer imagined Russian fighters to look like, the results were not really convincing.

By 1949 most F-47s serving in regular Air Force units had been replaced, but with the outbreak of the Korean War in 1950 it was decided that whereas the F-51 would be a useful ground support machine operating in company with jet types, the F-47 could fill a training requirement in the fighter squadrons of the Air National Guard. Eventually 28 ANG squadrons were equipped with Thunderbolts, primarily late-model Ds and Ns. This latter service extended the operational life of the F-47 into the early 1950s but most had been replaced by mid-decade.

3. Thunderbolt People: Engineers and Aces

During the various design exercises that led utimately to the P-47, Alexander Kartveli's expertise as an engineer led to the incorporation of several novel features. The most challenging task was to shoehorn a turbocharger into the fuselage, but there was one other that was also not that obvious externally. In order to persuade the landing gear of the XP-47 to be completely enclosed by doors when fully retracted, a telescopic strut was fitted. This automatically extended the gear by 9 in (22.86 cm) when it was lowered, an arrangement that allowed adequate clearance for the 12-ft (3.66 m) diameter propeller. This four-bladed unit was the first of its kind fitted to any US fighter and the compressing-strut landing gear avoided the need to adapt the wing design. An oddity, one that was quite fashionable at the time, was the 'car door' type entry to the cockpit. Also fitted on the Bell P-39 and never changed, this cumbersome arrangement was eliminated on the P-47 in favour of a sliding cockpit canopy that was found to be more convenient.

So much was at stake as Lowery Brabham taxied out for the first flight of the XP-47 that there must have been more than a few anxious people among the crowd of employees who turned out to witness the event on that May day in 1941. Brabham duly took off, made a number of passes over the airfield and executed enough manoeuvres to show that all the work over the preceeding months had been worth it. Brabham's comments on landing were very positive.

Despite the fact that Kartveli had designed the largest fighter in the world, given it a battery of machine guns of unprecedented hitting power – and indirectly staked Republic's future on the new design being a winner – it was the slide rules which had determined what was a very bold step. If it was to use the big Pratt & Whitney R-2800 engine and accommodate a turbocharger, the aircraft's outsize fuselage dimensions were decided almost from the start.

Another unique aspect of the design was to increase the permissible loaded weight specified in the Air Corps requirement from under 13,000 lb (5897 kg) for the XP-47 to more than 20,000 lb (9072 kg). Anticipating the usual weight spiral when what is known as government furnished equipment is added to any military aircraft, Kartveli had showed much foresight. He designed a fighter that was not only larger than any of its contemporaries, American or foreign, but which was strong enough to bear additional loads with ease. It remained something of gamble, because high weight compromised climb rate and manoeuvrability at low altitudes, but it was one that was to pay off handsomely.

Testing the P-47

Republic estimated that two years from maiden flight would be required to thoroughly test the XP-47B for safe operational use, which reflected not only how advanced a design it was but the unhurried pace of such things before the war. This time period was cut due mainly to two unforeseen events. One was the US declaration of war in December 1941, and the second took

Cass Hough, head of VIII Air Service Command, in the cockpit of a P-47 which, out of all the types he flew during the war, he tended to favour. He flew P-47D-1 (42-7921) so regularly that it became virtually his personal aircraft. (*Author*)

place on 8 August 1942. Taking the prototype aloft for a yet another attempt to persuade its engine to deliver 2,000 hp was Filmore 'Phil' Gilmore. Before the gear was even retracted the pilot noticed that the manifold pressure was about to pass the 'red line'. Knowing that he had little time before the engine seized, Gilmore prepared to bail out. With no response to his attempt to retrim the aircraft he jettisoned the car door and the canopy and jumped. As the XP-47B had exceeded 400 mph before he abandoned it, Gilmore was lucky to escape with his life. Some panels of his parachute had been torn away by wind blast but he floated down as the first Thunderbolt plunged into Long Island Sound. This test pilot's survival was lucky for Republic, for had Gilmore died the company would not have had his first hand input into the cause of the engine malfunction.

Wright Field Project Officer for the P-47 was Lt Col Mark E Bradley, who had flown the XP-47 for the first time on 1 January 1942. The prototype, fitted with eight 0.50-in (12.7 mm) machine guns, had been delivered to what was then Patterson Field the day previously. Bradley decided to use the WWI gun butts sited on the airfield for the initial tests. No flying was scheduled, the aircraft being wheeled in front of the butts and jacked up for firing. All did not go well. Bradley duly climbed into the cockpit and thumbed the firing button. After a few rounds the guns stopped. Dejected because this was one of the most urgent test programmes Wright had at that time, Bradley climbed down and examined the bays. He found that not only had all the guns jammed but some of the mounts had broken and the weapons had become dislodged.

The reason was that these particular guns had come from a new production source, which had not yet mastered the art of gun interchangeability and other tricks of the trade to make them operate reliably. A rapid 'fix' was initiated and there were few further problems with the Thunderbolt's main armament.

Female test pilot

Among the pilots who flew the P-47 was Wright Field-assigned WASP (Womens' Airforce Service Pilots) Anne Carl Baumgartner. She reported that the aircraft was so heavy that after a climb to altitude and completion of the scheduled test, the fuel was almost exhausted and most landings were little more than the dead-stick variety.

Included in the list of unsung contributors to the history of the P-47 were the engineers at Pratt & Whitney. In the summer of 1942, in response to performance figures published for the FW 190, Opie Chenoweth, head of the Army's Technical Service Command, discussed this matter with T E Ellinghast, P&W's aircraft sales manager. The fact that had raised eyebrows in America was the German fighter's outstanding rate of climb, which took only 4 minutes and 45 seconds to reach 16,500 ft (5029 m). This was more than a match for the XP-47, which required more than five minutes to reach 15,000 ft (4572 m), a figure that would steadily be eroded as weight was added to production Thunderbolts.

By incorporating a system whereby water-methanol was injected into the cylinders, the P-47D-11 showed a significant increase in performance, an attribute enhanced by fitting a paddle-blade propeller. (*Republic*)

Ellinghast believed that the R-2800-21 in the P-47 could deliver more power and thereby match enemy performance – if only the problem of premature fuel detonation could be solved. Pratt & Whitney had, fortuitously, filed patents in 1938 for an anti-detonation injection method using water, and a team headed by Perry Pratt, project engineer for the R-2800, began work on a trial system. Within three months the first kits had been installed on P-47Ds based in Europe; combat pilots were highly appreciative of the extra boost of 40 mph (64.4 km/h) coupled with the better rate of climb that the injection system provided.

This WEP or War Emergency Power modification was first installed as standard on the R-2800-63 'B' series engine, but the R-2800-21 could have the equipment retrofitted, in which case it was redesignated as a 'dash 63' powerplant. Fitted as a standard item of

equipment from the P-47D-20 onwards, water injection automatically gave the aircraft a 'sling-shot' burst of speed when the pilot pushed the throttle lever one-eighth of an inch past its normal maximum travel. Coupled with the later fitting of a 13-ft (3.96 m) diameter Curtiss Electric propeller with paddle blades which improved cooling, the T-bolt enjoyed a brief boost of power amounting to 15 per cent, pushing engine horsepower up to 2,535 and maximum speed to 433 mph (697 km/h).

Thoroughly determining the reliability of the R-2800's water injection system required the services of several Army fighter pilots seconded to Wright Field for that purpose. Among them were Gabe Vacca, Arnold Benson, Roy Saux, and Lieutenants Pavlovic and Hebert.

Under strict orders not to indulge in aerobatics, these pilots began flying with instrumented P-47s carrying tanks holding

The mighty 18-cylinder Pratt & Whitney R-2800 Double Wasp two-row radial that powered all front-line P-47s was renowned as one of the finest piston-driven aero-engines ever built. Here, mechanics of the 324th Fighter Group are preparing to hoist this one out of a P-47D for major servicing. *(IWM)*

some 15 gal (12.9 Imp gal/56.8 l) of distilled water. This was injected into the carburettor as the aircraft reached full power on take-off. For the pilots the worst aspect of these tests was the requirement to write down everything that happened, as it happened. Airspeed, rate of climb, engine rpm and so on had to be faithfully recorded on take-off and at every 5,000 feet (1524 m) thereafter. With no radar or air traffic control to help, the pilots had also to ensure they kept out of each other's way in several flights a day for a period of months.

Many records were set and broken on these flights, including that for an aircraft's time to 10,000 ft (3048 m), but being wartime, all such data was classified. Republic could not believe the figures the AAF pilots were obtaining and sent its own pilots to verify them.

In the meantime the AAF test pilots were transferred to combat units. They all ended up in the 406th Fighter Group in time to accompany it to Europe as part of the 9th Air Force. Of those named above, Arnold Benson was killed in action on 16 June 1944, while Lt Pavlovic died in an accident before leaving.

Mention should also be made of another group of pilots vital to the success of the P-47 and virtually all other wartime aircraft, namely the ferry pilots. As more and more male civilian pilots enlisted in the armed forces, so women answered the call to fill out the vacancies. WASPs ferried aircraft across the US for onward shipment to the combat groups overseas. One of the ladies associated with the P-47 was Teresa James. She flew *Ten Grand* away soon after the naming ceremony and

Francis 'Gabby' Gabreski was the leading 8th Air Force ace, with 28 victories, when he went down to ground fire on 10 July 1944 to join many of his comrades in a German PoW cage. He was startled to be welcomed by his captors almost as though he had been expected! Seen here with his ground crew, Gabby was lost in this P-47D-25 (42-26418). (S Blake)

delivered it to the docks at Newark, New Jersey where it left for Italy and the 79th Fighter Group. There the aircraft was flown by Lt Col Johnny Martin, Deputy Group CO on the 79th's 30,000th sortie in January 1945.

Field reps

Major Cass Hough, head of VIII Fighter Command Air Technical Section at Bovingdon, was among the first pilots to fly the P-47C in England. Hough is known to have made an evaluation flight as early as 23 January 1943

and in subsequent weeks he built up an invaluable data file on operating characteristics. What Hough found in the P-47 was much to his liking, but with some reservations about the C model's suitability for combat in Europe.

When the P-47 got into action Republic, in common with other US manufacturers, allocated field representatives to the different war theatres. Men such as Charles J Jacobie worked closely with the combat groups and placed themselves on call to answer questions, suggest 'fixes' for any technical problems that

Robert S Johnson just missed making top slot in the 56th by achieving 27 victories with the Wolfpack. He was America's fifth-ranking ace, after Bong, McGuire, McCampbell and Gabreski. (*IWM*)

Donovan F Smith became an ace flying with the 61st FS, 56th Fighter Group. His score stood at five and a half victories at the end of the war. (*Conger/Blake*)

arose in combat, or recommended more drastic action. They had the authority to order aircraft to be taken out of service pending remedial attention at service depots which were better equipped for the task than unit-level maintenance echelons. That said, the combat units became adept at solving many problems and challenges that would otherwise have kept too many P-47s on the ground at vital times. P-47 groups could also call on the trouble-shooting expertise of representatives from the engine and propeller manufacturers as well as Republic.

Thunderbolt aces

The WWI practice of bestowing the status of ace on a pilot who had destroyed five of the enemy in aerial combat was soon rekindled in the second war. Even before US pilots got into action on 7 December 1941 members of the

Eagle Squadrons in England had 'reinvented' the term, the RAF providing the means to that end. But as many of the Eagles found, becoming an ace could be far from easy when the enemy remained scarce and the weather was terrible. When the 8th Air Force began sending fighter groups to England in the spring of 1943, pilots naturally wondered if someone could better the score of 26 achieved by Eddie Rickenbacker, the top American ace in WWI.

That Republic had provided the means to repeat that success in Europe was demonstrated once the P-47 was operational with several groups. It was therefore doubly frustrating that for months the *Luftwaffe* failed to appear in force to fully test the theory of fighters being able to effectively protect bombers. But the way the air war over Europe was shaping up appeared to offer many chances for individual US pilots to score

Paul Conger was one of more than 40 pilots who made ace while flying with the 56th Fighter Group. Current research places his score with the group at 11.5. He finished the war flying the P-47M. *(Conger/Blake)*

victories. For one thing, their adversaries were occupied almost exclusively in attacking bombers without – to use a hunting simile – much need to flush them out. On bad days, scores of enemy fighters attacked the bombers. For the P-47 pilots there remained the problem of getting to grips with the agile German interceptors so they could make a significant difference by reducing bomber losses.

Following weeks of largely inconclusive clashes with the *Jagdwaffe*, pilots of P-47s with extra fuel tanks began to score aerial victories. The totals were modest at first, and occasionally offset by the loss of similar numbers of American fighters on some frustrating missions. Then the rise of the European Theatre aces began with Capt Charles London of the 78th Group who shot

down his fifth enemy aircraft on 29 June 1943.

While there was no denying London his achievement as the first AAF ace in the 8th Air Force, Col Hub Zemke's 56th Group, the most experienced P-47 outfit, was obliged to grit its collective teeth until the summer. Then the original P-47 group could announce Gerald W Johnson as its first ace, the beginnings of a string of successes leading to a highly respectable final score in what was rated as the toughest war theatre of all.

There followed an illustrious list – Robert Johnson, Francis Gabreski, Dave Schilling, Fred Christensen, Walker Mahurin, Gerald Johnson, Joe Powers, Leroy Schreiber, Felix Williamson and Michael Quirk as well as Zemke himself. These men became the war's 'top ten' aces in the 56th, all with double-figure scores. And they were only a handful of the eventual 100-plus aces who flew as part of the Wolfpack, the group destroying 677 enemy aircraft in aerial combat during the war.

While the Wolfpack's achievements were synonymous with the P-47 because the unit flew no other aircraft type in combat, scores of other pilots began their personal victory tallies on the P-47 before passing to the P-38 or P-51, depending on the theatre. This was particularly true of the 8th Air Force, which gradually moved on from the P-47 and P-38 during 1944 and 1945. In other theatres it was most likely that pilots had started their record of victories on the P-40 before transferring to a P-47 group or staying with their original unit when it was re-equipped with Thunderbolts.

Tactical aces

Even though the 9th Air Force P-47 groups were primarily tasked with ground attack missions, they still had a sprinkling of aces and several who just missed the magic five. The 362nd Group's Edwin Fisher claimed seven victories as the tactical force's top ace, with Robert Coffey of the 365th coming second with six. These two groups scored a close total of 121 and 121.5 air victories respectively to round out in second and third place in the overall 9th AAF listing. The top-scoring 9th AAF group was the 368th with 129 kills.

The above figures show the disparity in the number of victories achieved by the different circumstances in which the P-47 fighter groups of the 8th and 9th Air Forces were deployed. In the latter force shooting at enemy aircraft until attacked was positively discouraged, at least in some units, and the odd official method of recording claims as 'unconfirmed destroyed' muddied the waters to the extent that individual pilots who were one or two kills short of ace sought confirmation of their shooting ability for years after the war.

A chance to score aerial victories was a bonus for the 9th Air Force. Trained in ground attack work, pilots found themselves escorting heavies, the official view being that there could never be any such thing as too many fighters to cover the bombers. Some units suspected that during the pre-D-Day period the 9th's fighters were being treated as a poor relation to the 8th and were handed the less attractive chore of

Joe Powers was another 56th 'Wolfpack' ace, scoring 12 kills with the 61st Fighter Squadron and another 2.5 with the 62nd FS. (Conger/Blake)

withdrawal support. Nevertheless, for many of the pilots, the possibility of combat with the *Luftwaffe* was enough to dispel any feeling of being 'second-best'.

The great bulk of P-47 victims in 1943 and 1944 were German fighters, but individual scores were occasionally made up by bombers, transports or trainers. When American fighters operated *en masse* over the continent, airfield attacks found enemy aircraft in the landing pattern and others which had just become airborne. Picking these off represented a legitimate aerial victory.

Jet menace

During what turned out to be the last winter of the war, several pilots of the AAF tactical groups made contact with the revolutionary Messerschmitt Me 262. Well aware of the existence of jet and rocket interceptors that made the P-47 and all its kin obsolete, the Allies had cause to worry. But as subsequent events showed, the *Luftwaffe* failed to deploy the jet fighter in numbers high enough to exploit its

Highest-scoring ace of the crack 354th Fighter Group was Glenn Eagleston. In common with other pilots he bemoaned the change from the P-51 to the P-47 in the winter of 1944, but that did not stop him having his 18.5 victories plus his trademark eagle insignia painted on his personal Thunderbolt.

superior qualities, and the Me 262 began to fall victim to its 'outdated' Allied opponents.

On 1 November 1944, Lt Walter R Groce of the 63rd Squadron met the future along with a group of P-51s. Heading the Me 262 away from the bombers it was intent on attacking, Groce got in some telling strikes from a deflection shot, setting the starboard turbojet on fire. Following the stricken jet down, the P-47 pilot saw the German occupant bail out. As the Mustangs had also fired at the Me 262 Groce was awarded only a half credit but this initial encounter answered many questions about the performance of the German jet compared to that of the two top AAF fighters.

By early 1945 the chance to become an ace while flying a Thunderbolt was becoming increasingly rare, at least in Europe. The decimation of the *Luftwaffe*, and the dominance of the P-51 on the long-range escort missions

where the enemy could still be found, meant that the scoreboards of the tactical Thunderbolt groups remained largely similar to those of early 1944. Targets were road, rail and river transport, airfields, marshalling yards, gun emplacements and enemy strongpoints of all types, and not an accumulation of victories through aerial combat.

But in line with VIII Fighter Command's confirmation that enemy aircraft destroyed on the ground would be credited to individual pilots and make some of them 'ground aces' the groups made more records as fuel shortages began to bite the *Luftwaffe*. Allied fighter bomber pilots ran across airfields chock-full of aircraft in 1945, and just in case the enemy proved capable of mounting another *Bodenplatte*-type operation the P-47 and P-51 groups went on strafing sprees and came home with scores of ground victories to ensure that the bulk of the *Luftwaffe* was finally neutralised. Most pilots did not consider the results to be in the same league as aerial victories but strafing defended airfields was recognised as the most dangerous form of ground attack there was. Those whose gun cameras confirmed their shooting ability to back the claims they filed received due credit.

Mediterranean T-bolts

Six 12th/15th Air Force fighter groups and the two fighter bomber groups which had flown the A-36 converted to the P-47 in the MTO from late 1943 into early 1944. With the creation of the 15th Air Force, the 325th and 332nd plus three groups of P-38s were to handle bomber escort, both the former later switching to the P-51. Before it did so the Checkertails produced six aces, the list being led by Herschel H Green, who scored ten while flying a razorback P-47D – as did all the other pilots. No bubbletop T-bolts were delivered to the group before it transitioned onto the P-51 in 1944. Close behind Green (who eventually brought his war total to eighteen) were Eugene H Emmons and George P Novotny with nine and eight respectively. All these pilots flew in the 317th Squadron.

Ground attack took on a higher priority as the *Luftwaffe* faded from Mediterranean skies. Delivering hundreds of tons of bombs and rockets into narrow railway cuttings to block tunnels, wreck locomotives and disable rolling

Lt Col Robert L Coffey revs up *Coffey's Pot* – his personal P-47D – as he prepares to take off from Beaulieu, Hants on D-Day. Then attached to the 365th Group headquarters, he previously flew combat missions with the 388th Squadron. This aircraft was shot down later in 1944. (*Crow*)

stock, all tactical groups, including the 27th and 86th which had previously flown the A-36, were flying Thunderbolts by late 1944. Aerial combat still came the way of these groups but occasions similar to 2 April 1945, when the 350th Fighter Group routed an *Aeronautica Nazionale Repubblicana* (ANR) formation to the tune of 13 Bf 109s downed, occurred all too rarely for the pilots involved.

Fifth and Seventh Air Forces

With the inherent safety factor of possessing two engines, the P-38 was the one fighter that 5th Air Force commanding general George C Kenney wanted for his squadrons taking the war to the Japanese in New Guinea during 1943. Kenney would eventually get his Lightnings in abundance, but in mid-1943 he got the 358th Fighter Group with razorback P-47Ds. Unwilling to turn down anything capable of combat, Kenney did not protest despite his

doubts about deploying a single-engined fighter over the long distances involved in the theatre. As the first unit equipped with the Republic fighter in the SWPA, the 358th fought its way up the New Guinea island chain, numerous combats producing several aces apart from Neel Kearby. They included William R Rowland, Bill D Dunham, Lawrence O'Neill and John T Moore.

Razorback P-47Ds were retained until early in 1945, when the 358th was operating over the Philippines *en route* to becoming, in terms of aces, the most successful P-47 outfit in the Pacific. In the meantime the 35th and 58th Groups, the other two units flying early-model P-47Ds in the SWPA, had been similarly making their mark against the Japanese.

Having pitched into the battle for Saipan, the 7th Air Force's 318th Group flew very-short-range ground attack missions for weeks. Countering increasingly desperate attempts by

Major Herschel 'Herky' Green's final score of 18 – ten gained on the P-47 – placed him at the top of the list of 15th AF aces. Flying with the 317th Fighter Squadron of the 325th FG 'Checkertails', Green was the top-scoring Thunderbolt ace in the MTO. The six leading Checkertail aces all flew in the same squadron. (*USAF*)

Bob Baseler was another ace in the 325th, his final score flying the P-47 and P-51 being six. *(IWM)*

the Japanese to keep the island out of American hands did not bring about much air combat, and pilots such as eventual 6-victory ace William Mathis had to wait until the group was later re-equipped with the P-47N before scoring all his kills.

Philippine campaign

When in 1944 the drive across the Pacific shifted the focus of combat north to the Philippines, the 5th Air Force P-47 groups were transferred there to continue a protracted mopping-up campaign that was to last virtually until the end of the war. Equipped by then with some bubbletop P-47Ds, the 35th Group was moved to Luzon early in 1945. By then Capt Alvaro Jay Hunter of the group's 40th Squadron had destroyed three Oscars to round out his total score of five, the earlier two

victories falling during the unit's P-39 period. Edward R Hoyt, an ace in the 35th Group's 41st Squadron, had reached four the previous March with four Oscars. Hoyt's Betty kill while flying a P-47N on 13 August 1945 made it number five.

A shortage of P-38s had earlier seen squadrons of the 8th and 49th Fighter Groups convert to Thunderbolts amid, it has to be said, howls of protest. These died down as the P-47 demonstrated an ascendency over almost all Japanese aircraft likely to be met in combat. Maj Gerald R Johnson, 9th FS CO, shot down two enemy aircraft before the P-38 replacements arrived. He scored another 20 kills with the Lightning.

'Ace in a day'

Going out on a morning or afternoon mission and coming home an ace with five aerial victories – or indeed adding five to an existing score – was a heady accomplishment, one not shared by a great number of AAF pilots and usually celebrated by awards. Several P-47 pilots in the 5th, 7th and 8th Air Forces claimed such honours.

The first P-47 'ace in a day' in the 8th Air Force was the 56th's Capt Robert J Rankin who downed his five on 12 May 1944. Fred Christensen's aerial massacre of a gaggle of Ju 52 transports on 7 July 1944 was followed up by five downed by Dave Schilling in December and Felix Williamson in January 1945.

By the time the P-47N groups of the 7th Air Force had hit their stride on missions from Ie Shima, the chance to tangle with the enemy was no longer guaranteed. But the 318th Group more than got its chance on 25 May 1945 when Lt Richard H Anderson became an ace. Three days later this feat was repeated by the 318th's Capt John E Vogt. Both pilots were awarded the Distinguished Service Cross. World War II's last Army Air Force ace in a day – and the last ace of the war – was Lt Oscar F Perdomo, flying a P-47N. On 13 August his flight was patrolling off the coast of Korea when a number of Ki-43s was observed. In separate actions, Perdomo shot down four Oscars and an unfortunate Yokosuka K5Y Willow trainer that stumbled into his sights. Perdomo made no mistake and turned for home with five down. He too was awarded the DSC.

A busy scene, almost certainly at Burtonwood in Lancashire in 1944. Burtonwood was the main UK depot for repair and supply of aircraft to the 8th and 9th Air Forces. The fighter taking centre stage is a P-47D-27. A year later there would have been similar scenes at air bases all over the world, as with the end of the war the Thunderbolt was rapidly phased out of operational service and units disbanded. (*USAF*)

With the war over, the phase-out of the P-47 began, but at home there was still work for the aces. This usually involved a stint of pilot and gunnery training, although Robert Baseler, ex-CO of the Checkertails, undertook a different form of flying. Decking out a P-47D-28, a sub-type he had not actually flown in combat, Baseler contributed to an AAF recruitment drive. In the years immediately following the war the mass release of personnel had created acute shortages in the new USAF command structure. Baseler's P-47 and other aircraft acting as flying billboards did their bit to help.

In similar vein to the flying recruiters, Wright Field retained at least one P-47D-40 (45-49329)

after the war and applied high-visibility panels to contrast large notices. These warned aircraft without radios – known as NORDO traffic – entering the area to give the experimental base a wide berth. This was vital in a period when jet-powered test speeds were spiralling upwards, a fact not widely appreciated by civilian pilots.

Pilotless drones also represented a potential hazard to the unwary and a 'scarecrow' aircraft was an effective way of clearing the air. Seeing a big, beefy Thunderbolt bearing down on you with the words 'Clear Wright Field Area' emblazoned on its fuselage probably brought about a pretty rapid compliance!

4. P-47 Accomplishments: Performance and Users

Being thrust into the role of escort to long-range bombers was not exactly what Republic had envisaged for the P-47. No one had really thought about that idea or the problems involved. In fact, few AAF air chiefs had much idea of how single-seat fighters would be deployed in combat and some questioned the need for them at all, even after it had been clearly demonstrated that without such support a heavy bombing campaign was doomed if not to total failure then to high cost.

When VIII Fighter Command began operations from England, the planners found that the P-47 did not have the range needed to match that of the P-38, and there was no provision for it to carry external fuel tanks as a standard item of military equipment. Nevertheless, to offset a shortage of Lightnings, the Thunderbolt was the only American fighter available that could undertake this vital task and have a chance of surviving combat in hostile skies.

Fortunately the P-47 coped magnificently within the limitations of a large and thirsty engine, high weight and some performance limitations, holding the line until it could be supported, and in due course largely replaced, by the P-51. But in March 1943, as the first Thunderbolts prepared for their debut mission, that time was some way off.

Psychologically, the appearance of American fighters in the ETO did much for the morale of bomber crews. P-47s could take them up to the German border, further than the RAF's Spitfires had been able to do. That fact alone was highly appreciated and knowing that, even if the unescorted part of the mission had been gruelling, their own fighters would be up to shepherd the cripples back over the Channel was a comforting reassurance. It was said that even seeing the fighters turning back at their range limitation point was not the traumatic event it might have seemed to the crews of the 'Big Friends'. The bomber boys knew that within a few hours their 'Little Friends' would be back with them. But the AAF planners were to be made forcibly aware by several headline-grabbing extreme-range missions in 1943 that the real answer to conducting a heavy bomber campaign in daylight against such opposition as the *Luftwaffe* represented, was 'all the way' fighter escort. Individually, the 'self defending' bomber was shown to be little more than a myth; tight formations maintained at all times could to some extent deter fighter attacks and minimise bomber casualties. But a protective screen of fighters was the real answer.

Air-to-air

When it came to aerial combat, the P-47 proved more than capable of holding its own and meting out destruction. An armament of eight heavy machine guns had seemed a little excessive to some of the early P-47 pilots, who felt that the designers were thus implying that they were unable to shoot accurately and needed to 'hose' the target with fire in order to bring it down. While in some instances that was undoubtedly true, the P-47D's heavy armament was a good compromise between the lighter, 0.30-in (7.62 mm) machine gun and the even heavier 20-mm cannon. The weight of fire under the pilot's thumb was insurance even for the novice, and in close encounters with less robustly built enemy fighters the P-47 proved superior on countless occasions.

In terms of field maintenance, machine guns proved marginally more reliable than cannon which had a tendency to jam. A Browning also carried a greater number of rounds per gun than a cannon, the P-47's battery totalling 3,400 rounds, up to 425 rounds per gun. This proved adequate on most missions likely to involve air-to-air combat: time and again the eight 'fifties of a P-47 brought down the *Luftwaffe*'s Bf 109 and FW 190 with ease, not to mention the Bf 110 and Me 410. Against all the leading German fighters the Thunderbolt performed well, the results of several well placed bursts of fire often proving disastrous to the enemy aircraft.

Unexpected need

The distance the P-47 could or could not cover from bases in southern England soon became something of a political issue. Washington was screaming for bomber losses to be reduced, and for fighters to knock down far more of the enemy than was possible in mid-1943.

Republic had placed all the P-47's fuel in fuselage tanks and had originally made no provision for the aircraft to carry additional fuel, for example, in internal wing tanks. But the carriage of external tanks soon became a vital necessity. Thrust into supporting an air war that had become the yardstick by which all other USAAF bombing operations would be judged, the P-47 squadrons in England began filling a hitherto unappreciated need in military aviation, that of the single-seat fighter with unprecedented range.

Achieving this with a single-engined aircraft had appeared all but impossible before the war began; British Air Staff advisers cautioned against pursuing such a concept while their American opposite numbers placed all their faith in the 'self-defending' bomber. If an escort fighter was needed, it was believed that two engines were *de rigueur*, and only the P-38 Lightning could take on that role.

But with P-38s committed heavily to North Africa after Operation *Torch* and theatre commanders in the Pacific pleading for every one off the production line, the 8th Air Force had, temporarily, to take a back seat.

In the light of shortages and general complacency, it fell to Republic to bring together all the variables – weight, power settings, altitude, weather conditions, combat time – and push the P-47 ever further. This the company did, raising the 'normal' range of the P-47D-1 from 400 miles (644 km) at 25,000 ft (7620 m) to 590 miles (950 km) for the P-47D-25 and finally to 800 miles (1288 km) for the P-47N-1 operating at the same height. The respective ferry range figures for these three models were 825 miles (1328 km), 1,030 miles (1658 km) and 2,000 miles (3219 km), the majority of figures being obtained at a similar altitude although the P-47D-25 covered this distance flying at 10,000 ft (3048 m).

As things turned out, the all-embracing faith in the P-38 fell short when the aircraft issued to the 8th Air Force suffered more than others at the hands of the weather. By late 1943 the P-47 had carved its own niche as the original escort fighter, a position it held briefly until the P-51 overshadowed it in this respect. But it could never lose the accomplishment of being the first fighter capable of taking on the *Luftwaffe* over territory it had hitherto considered its own.

More fuel, more weight

The ability of the P-47 to carry more fuel and ordnance was not bought without a weight/performance penalty. It was fortunate that the original airframe had been 'stretched' to accommodate the R-2800 engine because this enabled the aircraft to soak up extra loads without any critical loss of performance.

The one drawback of the P-47 was its inability to climb fast, particularly with a full load, a difficulty compounded if available runway length was compromised. In the Pacific, pilots flying the P-47N from the island of Ie Shima on occasion found this problem to be acute. It was a tribute to the design that it usually coped, even in marginal operating conditions. These included areas notorious for high humidity levels, where the leaden air sometimes led to a frightening tendency of the aircraft failing to unstick, as the runway boundary loomed.

An illustration of the weight spiral versus performance dilemma, one faced by most designers of combat aircraft, can be made by comparing the 'first and last' P-47s: at a gross

Ammunition-loading via the large upper wing doors of the P-47 rarely gave squadron armourers any serious problems. Hanging below them is a 500-lb (227 kg) general purpose (GP) bomb. (*IWM*)

Bombs of various types could be carried by the P-47. Seen here is a fairly typical combination of two 500-pounders with a single centreline 108-gal drop tank. (*IWM*)

weight of 12,086 lb (5482 kg) the XP-47B had a top speed of 412 mph (663 km/h) whereas the highly developed P-47N-1 at 16,300 lb (7394 kg) gross reached 467 mph (751.6 km/h). This represented a speed gain of just 55 mph (88.5 km/h) over the entire P-47 model series.

But such figures can be misleading. Under a mass of other considerations that dictate aircraft performance, the reality was that US fighters were outstandingly successful under most operating conditions.

If positive reasons are sought for the success of the P-47, it is worth recording that wartime pilot narratives often quote a combination of water injection and paddle-blade propellers as the two main attributes that Republic built into the P-47. These, more than any other technical advance enabled the Thunderbolt to improve its manoeuvrability as well as its low-altitude acceleration to the point where P-47 pilots had little cause to fear any adversary. Flying in 'clean' condition the P-47D could take on the enemy's best at all altitudes and if necessary break off combat to initiate that phenomenal

diving acceleration for which the big Republic fighter was rightly famous.

Fighter tactics

By the time the P-47 entered combat in Europe, fighter tactics had undergone a fundamental change. No longer did pilots adopt photographically impressive but inherently dangerous 'V' and echelon formations. The Germans had shown that the only way pilots of high-speed fighters could watch the sky without constant fear of a mid-air collision was to adopt the 'finger four' formation, with a wingman staying close at all times and which allowed pairs to manoeuvre around each other safely while taking on the enemy. This classic formation, which offered maximum flexibility, was universally adopted and it proved sound in all situations.

Fighting leaders such as the 56th Group's Hub Zemke were among those who devised battle tactics tailored to the capability of the P-47. Aiming to put as many of his pilots as possible into contact with the *Luftwaffe*, this

The belly of *Princess Pat* held a nasty surprise for ground-based infantry targets, in the form of a clutch of 20 small fragmentation bombs. The aircraft was part of the Wolfpack's 63rd Fighter Squadron. (*Aeroplane*)

popular leader devised his 'Zemke Fan'. Briefly, this involved the group flying ahead of the bombers to a given area then breaking into separate flights over a 180 degree arc to cover the largest possible section of sky. Its main purpose was to catch the *Luftwaffe* fighters before they could form up to attack the US heavies. An extra section of P-47s flew in the centre, primed to go to the aid of others in contact with the enemy. The Zemke Fan worked well on its first trial on 12 May 1944, the result being 18 victories for the loss of three Thunderbolts.

If further proof is needed that the P-47 was a deadly weapon in the USAAF arsenal, a closer look at the combat record of the Wolfpack more than confirms it. As the most experienced P-47

unit in combat anywhere, the unit's pilots regularly led the list of 8th Air Force aces. Apart from normal tour-expired rotations home, it was bad luck and deadly enemy ground fire rather than any failure of the Thunderbolt that steadily removed them from the scene.

Ground attack techniques

As a fighter bomber the P-47 also had few peers. Much had been learned from the first 8th Air Force P-47 dive bombing mission which had taken place on 25 November 1943. It was found, for, example that the difficulty in persuading the P-47 to pull out of a high-speed dive meant that a much shallower approach was advisable. On that occasion each aircraft carried a pair of 500-lb (227 kg) fragmentation

Although fairly cumbersome, the M-10 triple launcher for 4.5-in HVAR or High Velocity Air Rockets could be an effective weapon if the P-47 pilot got the hang of aiming – though that could prove tricky. Not everyone took to the weapon, but it could be devastating in the right hands. (*IWM*)

bombs to attack a French airfield, these being released at around 10,000 feet (3048 m) after diving 5,000 ft (1524 m). Another lesson, one driven home rather than coming as a surprise, was that if alerted, German flak was deadly and accurate. In sum, similar attacks in the future would be initiated from 15,000 ft (4572 m) with bomb release between 10,000 and 7,000 ft (2134 m), dive angles being varied according to enemy reaction and the degree of surprise

achieved. This last was significant. If the attack could commence without the enemy reacting fast enough, considerable damage would usually result – with minimum loss to the attacking force.

With its heavy gun armament the P-47 was a 'natural' at ground strafing. Unrivalled in its ability to destroy all types of ground target, Thunderbolts could also withstand attention by the flak better than most other Allied fighters –

Carrying the as yet unexplained code 'J17', this P-47D was used in the extensive trials designed to verify HVAR rockets for service. The split combination became standard on P-47s, although tiered-type launchers carrying up to 16 rounds were tried out. (MAP)

but more than one pilot was lost because he tried to hug the ground that bit too closely and touched the tips of the propeller blades. But even when his aircraft was brought down as a result of such an incident, the pilot often walked away from the wreckage without serious injury.

As the Allied armies made the breakout from the Normandy bridgehead the Thunderbolt groups of the 9th came into their own. Having planned for close air support to be as accurate and as free of 'friendly fire' mistakes as was possible, various steps had been taken.

Experienced pilots acting as air-ground controllers rode in tanks, armoured cars or half-tracks to call in the fighter bombers by radio. These men were fully aware of the destructive power (and limitations) of the ordnance carried by the P-47s and other fighter bombers they controlled. They were also well versed in the skills required to aim bombs using the gunsight plus a few of their own techniques such as marking dive angles on a cockpit window. The lack of anything more sophisticated than a

gunsight appears not to have been a drawback; US fighter pilots generally proved themselves highly adept at destroying any type of enemy target, from trains and flak positions to barges and horse-drawn wagons, often mere yards from friendly troops.

Comparative effect

AAF statisticians compiled detailed data on the effects of tactical bombing by heavy and medium bombers and fighter bombers, vis-à-vis target destruction and the dangers to friendly troops in near proximity. Not surprisingly the P-47 was voted the most effective against the smaller tactical targets. The praise Thunderbolt pilots received from the ground forces was unreservedly positive.

Without resort to any special weapons, tactical P-47s were able even to cripple tanks and self-propelled artillery by bouncing bullets and bombs off the ground to strike the vulnerable undersides, engines and tracks of enemy vehicles.

In situations where return fire could be

P-47N-5 44-88335 is seen with a full load of 4.5-in HVARs specially painted for film recording purposes during firing trials. The never published results of these trials would make interesting reading. (*Republic*)

expected to be heavy, pilots knew that the T-bolt could take a tremendous amount of punishment as well as dish it out. Aircraft would return home battered and torn by the effects of enemy fire and encounters with more passive items such as telegraph poles and trees that happened to get in the way of their low-level attacks.

As with many other pilots before them the black airmen of the 322nd FG could recount incidents that put everyone in awe of the P-47's great strength. One in particular seemed to defy most of the laws of gravity, aeronautics and physics – not necessarily in that order.

During a mission on 22 June 1944, Capt Robert B Treswell was lost along with two other 100th Squadron pilots when *en route* to Corsica. The three P-47s flew so low that they went into the Tyrrhenian Sea. Witnesses swore they saw Treswell's aircraft disappear, continue on submerged for about 50 feet then re-emerge from the water. Reckoning that Treswell,

realising his predicament, had frantically hauled back on the stick, other pilots reported that the Thunderbolt then zoomed up out of the water and flew over a wingman's aircraft before plunging back, taking the unfortunate Treswell to a watery grave.

Tough and sturdy

In Burma, RAF pilots witnessed the Thunderbolt's ability to fly through the topmost branches of trees with relative impunity if height had been misjudged. Though they hardly made a habit of this they nevertheless praised the designer's forethought in building such a sturdy fighter.

As the Allied advance across north-western Europe was consolidated, the 'on call' fighter bomber service to the ground troops was improved, rapid reaction time being essential in relieving pressure on friendly units and reducing casualties. Blasting numerous obstacles to the advance, the 9th Air Force's

The Oldsmobile company built 20-mm Hispano cannon under licence, mainly, in the case of the USAAF, for fitting into the P-38. The 78th FG tested a pair of such weapons slung externally on the wing racks of the P-47D, but no operational use ensued as the eight 50-calibre heavy machine guns proved to be quite adequate. (*USAF*)

P-47s often made the difference between a timely capture of an enemy position or a frustrating hold-up due to stubborn resistance. Being on the receiving end of a strafing attack by a flight of P-47s flying at zero feet with all 32 heavy machine-guns blazing was not very conducive to a brave riposte!

If the hell came from the other direction and hit the P-47, a resilient pilot could always fly it home *sans* engine. That happened to a 56th Group pilot flying a D-2 (42-8000) shortly after D-Day. Badly damaged over France, the aircraft flew out over the Channel where its entire engine fell away. Where the engine, cowling and prop should have been there was just space. But the T-bolt was high enough to glide on until, safely over England, the pilot thought he ought to land. This proved to be a little tricky as the aircraft was very tail-heavy and as he banged down in a meadow the whole tail sheared off. When the wreck came to rest the pilot could hardly believe he was unharmed.

A primary factor in the success of the P-47 as a fighter bomber in Europe was organisation and good ground-air communications. In 1944 several mobile MEW – Microwave Early Warning – radar sets were sent to France to improve the speed of reaction by fighter bombers to rapidly changing tactical requirements.

The other side of the coin in this respect was electronic jamming. Each side made great efforts to 'blind' the target acquisition ability of the other and numerous sites were pin-pointed and attacked. A significant contribution to this aspect of the war was the attack by the 362nd Fighter Group on a German jamming station at Feldburg in the Taunus Mountains on 2 March 1945. So effective was the bombing that the station remained off the air for the remaining nine weeks of the war.

Medals of Honor

There were surprisingly few Medal of Honor awards to fighter pilots in World War II. Understandably, America's highest award for

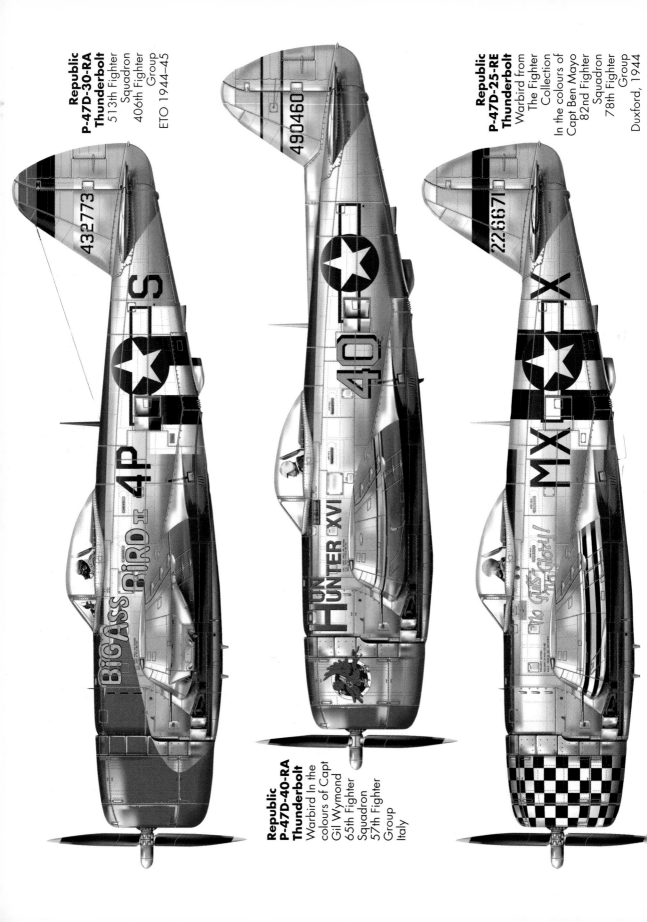

**Republic
P-47D-30-RA
Thunderbolt**
513th Fighter
Squadron
406th Fighter
Group
ETO 1944–45

432773

S

BiG ASS BiRD II 4P

**Republic
P-47D-25-RE
Thunderbolt**
Warbird from
The Fighter
Collection
In the colours of
Capt Ben Mayo
82nd Fighter
Squadron
78th Fighter
Group
Duxford, 1944

2226671

X

MX

No Guts No Glory!

490460

40

GUN HUNTER XVI

**Republic
P-47D-40-RA
Thunderbolt**
Warbird In the
colours of Capt
Gil Wymond
65th Fighter
Squadron
57th Fighter
Group
Italy

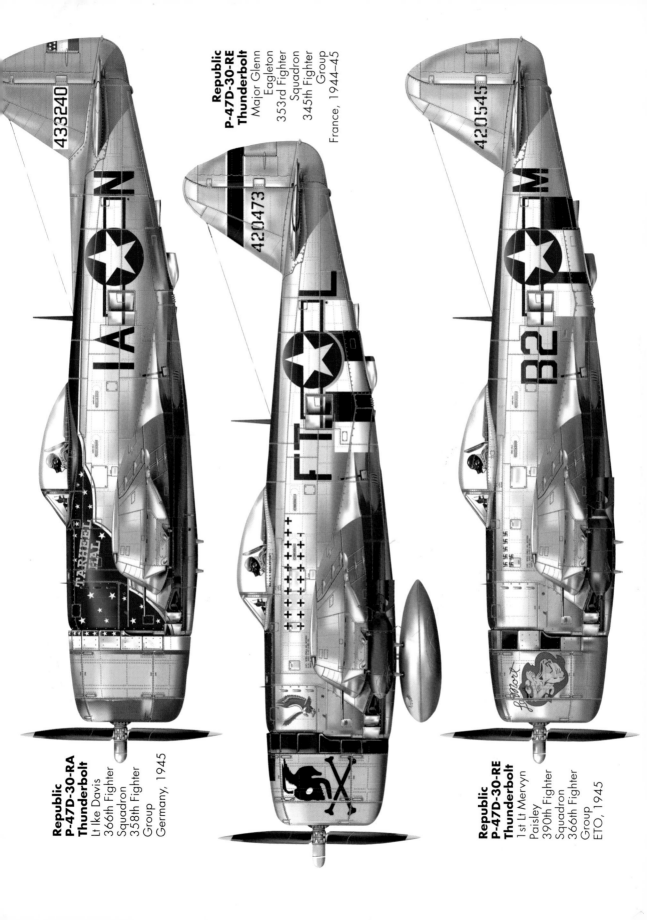

**Republic
P-47D-30-RA
Thunderbolt**
Lt Ike Davis
366th Fighter
Squadron
358th Fighter
Group
Germany, 1945

**Republic
P-47D-30-RE
Thunderbolt**
Major Glenn
Eagleton
353rd Fighter
Squadron
345th Fighter
Group
France, 1944–45

**Republic
P-47D-30-RE
Thunderbolt**
1st Lt Mervyn
Paisley
390th Fighter
Squadron
366th Fighter
Group
ETO, 1945

gallantry under fire was more reserved for singular acts of bravery where the inherent aggressiveness of the fighter pilot did not necessarily come directly into play. But there were exceptions. Of the two MoH awards to P-47 fighter pilots the second came more into this category.

On 25 April 1945 a P-47D 'Checkertail' of the 350th Fighter Group based at Pisa crashed in the foothills of the Apennines, taking the life of Lt Raymond Knight of the 346th Fighter Squadron. Riddled with bullets, Knight's aircraft had struggled to crest the mountain peaks, the pilot desperately trying to keep it airborne. The P-47D-27 (42-26785) had been hit by flak whilst Knight was strafing Bergamo airfield and his courageous but doomed attempt to return and save a valuable aircraft at a time when the group was short of replacements was rewarded by a posthumous Medal of Honor.

Jungle fighter

Becoming one of the few fighter pilots awarded the MoH for direct acts of outstanding combat prowess, Neel Kearby of the 348th Group joined a select band after an action on 11 October 1943. Heavily engaged with Japanese fighters east of Boram aerodrome, Kearby, flying a P-47D-2 (42-8145), shot down two Ki-61s and four Ki-43s although the latter, not unusually, were identified as Zekes or Hamps. Kearby's six victories and his exemplary leadership on this and other missions won him the Medal of Honor.

Kearby, a great advocate of the P-47, faced an unenviable task when his group was posted to the South West Pacific. Once again, heads were shaken in disbelief at the P-47's bulk and anticipated sluggishness in combat. And once again the critics were to be silenced.

By the time the 348th began combat operations in July 1943 the 5th Air Force had forced the Japanese firmly onto the defensive. Imperial fighter forces could use only three remaining bases – Wewak, Rabaul and Hollandia – to threaten the New Guinea area. Neel Kearby's run of victories reflected his tenacity and piloting skills but having run his score to 22, disaster struck on 5 March 1944. In combat with enemy bombers and fighters Kearby was shot down. He bailed out but was fatally injured in circumstances that were never fully explained as nobody saw his P-47D fall into the jungle. Neel Kearby was sorely missed by the 348th.

Second to none

By the end of the war all Allied squadrons equipped with the P-47 could congratulate themselves for a job well done. In all theatres the crippling losses in personnel and materiel inflicted on the Axis by Thunderbolt attack had reached staggering proportions. The units involved in this type of action had created the basis for an enduring postwar doctrine that would stretch far beyond that of bomber escort, a duty deemed so important in 1944–45. Yet when piston-engined heavy bomber fleets were very quickly rendered superfluous by the turbojet and atomic weapons, the fighter bomber would take on a new lease of life.

It was the squadrons that pioneered the concept of the escort fighter that gave the P-47 such an honourable and lasting place in aviation's hall of fame – but its true glory was gained by carrying out a different role. In striving for ever longer range to protect the heavy bombers the P-47 could not afford to fail; to the everlasting credit of its designers, engineers and pilots, it did not.

As good as the best

First-line fighters were subjected to numerous tests and comparisons during the war so that combat pilots could continue to receive the best aircraft the industry could provide. One such evaluation, the Joint Fighter Conference, took place at NAS Patuxent River, Maryland, on 16-20 October 1944. A board of experienced pilots examined the flight characteristics of the eight contemporary Army and Navy fighters (P-51D Mustang, F6F-5 Hellcat, F4U-4 Corsair, P-38L Lightning, P-61B Black Widow, P-63A Kingcobra and FM-2 Wildcat) placing their merits in order in more than 20 categories. Only then-current production models of each type were included, the Thunderbolt being represented by the P-47D-30.

The Republic fighter came top in five categories: best cockpit canopy; most comfortable cockpit; best all-around armour protection; best all-round fighter above 25,000 ft (7620 m) and best strafer. Just to emphasise

One of the best photos to come out of SEAC, this well-known view shows RAF Thunderbolt Mk IIs of No 30 Squadron, which had bright blue unit codes on their brown and green camouflage. (*IWM*)

how even informed opinions differ, the P-47 was rated fourth in the best all-around cockpit category and fifth in the worst all-around cockpit category! The P-47 also scored well in arrangement of engine controls, cockpit visibility and dive stability and control.

Everywhere it operated the P-47 had brooked no opposition, postwar analysis confirming what many already knew – that the Republic fighter had emerged as the most versatile all-round fighter bomber of the conflict. It said much for Alexander Kartveli's design expertise and the USAAC's faith in what was a bold concept in 1940. Lacking any real knowledge of how tactical airpower would develop under 'real war' conditions, the first big order laid the groundwork for development and continued success.

The balance sheet

Republic completed 15,683 Thunderbolts, two-thirds of which had found their way to combat zones and 5,222 aircraft were recorded as lost on active service. Further statistics from the air war included the fact that for every P-47 lost in aerial combat 4.9 enemy aircraft were claimed. The relative figures were 3,752 enemy aircraft shot down and 3,325 destroyed on the ground, with 824 P-47s lost to enemy aircraft, or a mere seven per cent of those flying combat. During its involvement in the fighting the P-47 flew 545,575 sorties, expended just under 135 million rounds of 0.50-in ammunition, fired 59,567 rockets and dropped 132,482 tons of bombs.

At the receiving end of all this firepower from D-Day to VE Day was every conceivable item of German materiel. In that period P-47s

**Republic P-47B
Thunderbolt**
Col Hubert Zemke
Commander, 56th Fighter Group
New York, 1942

16002

Republic Thunderbolt II
No 30 Squadron
Royal Air Force
Burma/India, 1944–45

RS C
KL308

**Republic P-47D-25-RE
Thunderbolt**
Lt Col Ken Gallup
350th Fighter Squadron
353rd Fighter Group
ETO 45

LH Q
226634

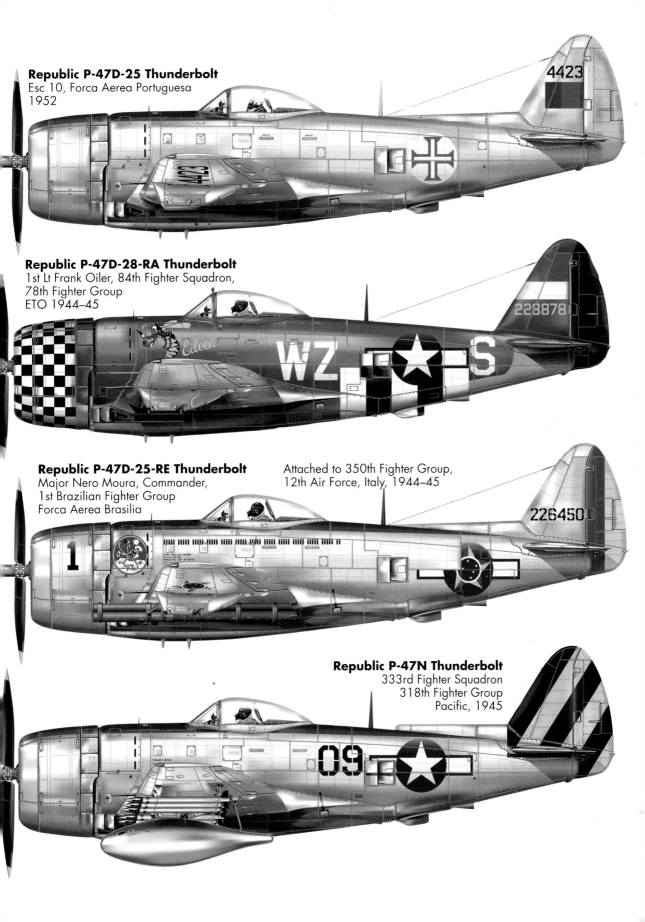

Republic P-47D-25 Thunderbolt
Esc 10, Forca Aerea Portuguesa
1952

4423

Republic P-47D-28-RA Thunderbolt
1st Lt Frank Oiler, 84th Fighter Squadron,
78th Fighter Group
ETO 1944–45

228878

Eileen

WZ ★ S

Republic P-47D-25-RE Thunderbolt
Major Nero Moura, Commander,
1st Brazilian Fighter Group
Forca Aerea Brasilia

Attached to 350th Fighter Group,
12th Air Force, Italy, 1944–45

226450

1

Republic P-47N Thunderbolt
333rd Fighter Squadron
318th Fighter Group
Pacific, 1945

09

Bolivia's only P-47 happened to be a rare D model that landed there and apparently stayed on the ground before being placed on a plinth! Bolivia never actually operated the P-47 although there was an apparent intention to do so. (*Merseyside Aviation Society*)

destroyed 9,000 locomotives, 8,600 items of rolling stock, 6,000 tanks and armoured vehicles and 6,800 trucks. By anyone's reckoning the achievements of pilots flying the P-47 were second to none.

Civilian work

Postwar civilian deployment of the P-47 was limited but it was tried out as a water bomber. With an on-going annual need to maintain a fleet of aircraft on immediate call to fight fires, the US Forest Service adapted two F-47Ns. Following tests at Eglin Field in mid-1947 and some actual sorties in Montana, the idea seemed to have merit. The Thunderbolts flew an initial sortie against fires in the western part of the state, releasing 165-gal tanks filled with water. On subsequent runs in company with a B-29 and a B-25, they dropped 56 tanks. But the fuel bill for two F-47s was found to be too high and an ambitious plan to deploy 75 fighters on fire suppression duty in 1948 came to nothing.

Overseas military duty

With peace and the formation of the USAF in 1947, aircraft designations were officially changed and the old 'P' for pursuit became 'F' for fighter. Postwar foreign users of the F-47 ran to an impressive list which included Brazil and Mexico, nations that had already seen active service flying Thunderbolts in WWII, while others were entirely fresh to the Republic fighter. Late-model F-47Ds and Ns met all postwar orders, several Latin-American air forces using the designation 'TF-47' to denote a training role.

To any such list Russia should be added and although little is known about P-47 use postwar, there were undoubtedly some remaining from Lend-Lease supplies. Russian-operated Thunderbolts were hardly, if ever, seen outside Soviet borders: no NATO reporting name was assigned, such being bestowed on virtually every Soviet-operated military aircraft, irrespective of origin.

Despite being an amalgam of several airframes, there is little to fault on the Fighter Collection's pristine P-47D kept in flying trim at Duxford, Cambridge – itself a former Thunderbolt base. (*Brian Marsh*)

Bolivia

Only one P-47 ever reached Bolivia despite an announced intention to standardise on the type during the late 1940s. The sole Thunderbolt, which arrived at El Alto air base in a very sorry state after a flight from Washington, was identified as a TP-47D-2-RE, famously the only razorback example in Latin-America. It is believed not to have been flown again but served out its days as an instructional airframe before becoming a monument at El Alto.

Brazil

The 1° *Grupo de Aviação de Caça* deployed alongside USAAF units in the European Theater of Operations and at the end of the war the group had flown 445 missions, 2,550 individual sorties and 5,465 combat flight hours in P-47Ds. After the war the *Grupo* re-equipped with 19 brand new P-47D-30-RAs, their old machines replacing P-40s operated by the 2° *Grupo de Caca*. A further 25 P-47s (soon to be redesignated F-47) were acquired in 1947. By the mid-1950s Brazil still had F-47s on strength, but few were serviceable. A rapidly increasing accident rate eventually brough operational flying to an end, and the type was retired in July 1957 after nearly 16 years of service.

Chile

The *Fuerza Aerea de Chile* received 48 F-47Ds Funded under the American Republics/ Military Defense Aid Program in September 1947. These were integrated into *Grupo de Aviacion* No 3, a large, mixed formation of ex-WWII aircraft. In 1949 the Thunderbolts formed a separate fighter unit, *Grupo* No 5 which was redesignated *Grupo* No 11. A low in-commission rate reduced the FACH F-47 inventory to one by late 1949 although this improved in 1952 when 14 F-47D-40s were received. Six years later jet equipment brought about the final phase-out of the venerable old Thunderbolts.

China

Although the majority of Chinese Air Force combat sorties during WWII were by types other than the P-47, the Nationalist regime was supplied with substantial quantities of Thunderbolts under Lend-Lease. These subsequently formed the 11th Fighter Group, which was expanded to wing strength with 40 aircraft in the air force order of battle for 1947. Relatively little air action is believed to have taken place between the two factions before mainland China fell to Communist forces. Re-

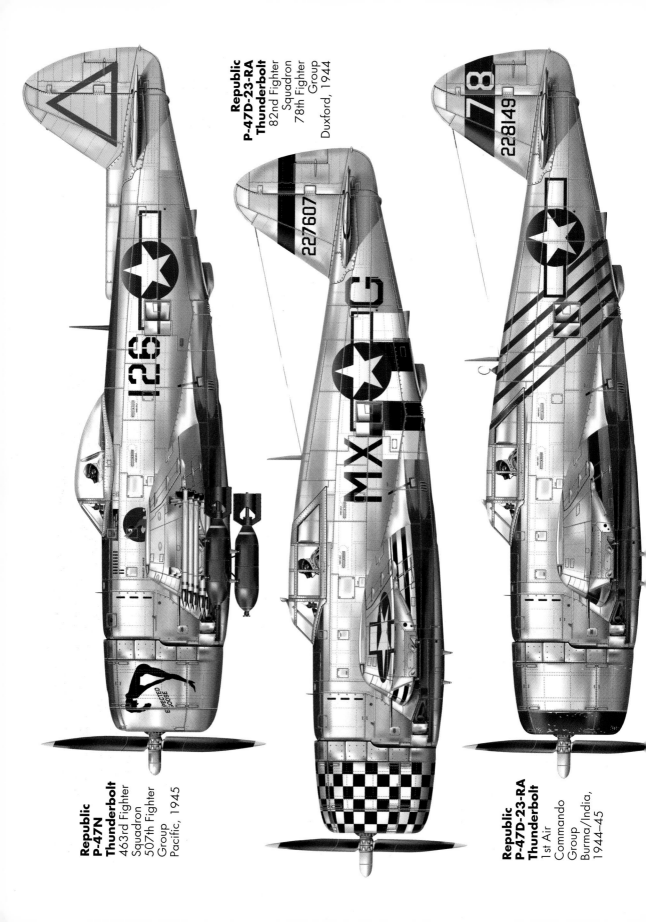

**Republic
P-47N
Thunderbolt**
463rd Fighter
Squadron
507th Fighter
Group
Pacific, 1945

**Republic
P-47D-23-RA
Thunderbolt**
82nd Fighter
Squadron
78th Fighter
Group
Duxford, 1944

**Republic
P-47D-23-RA
Thunderbolt**
1st Air
Commando
Group
Burma/India,
1944–45

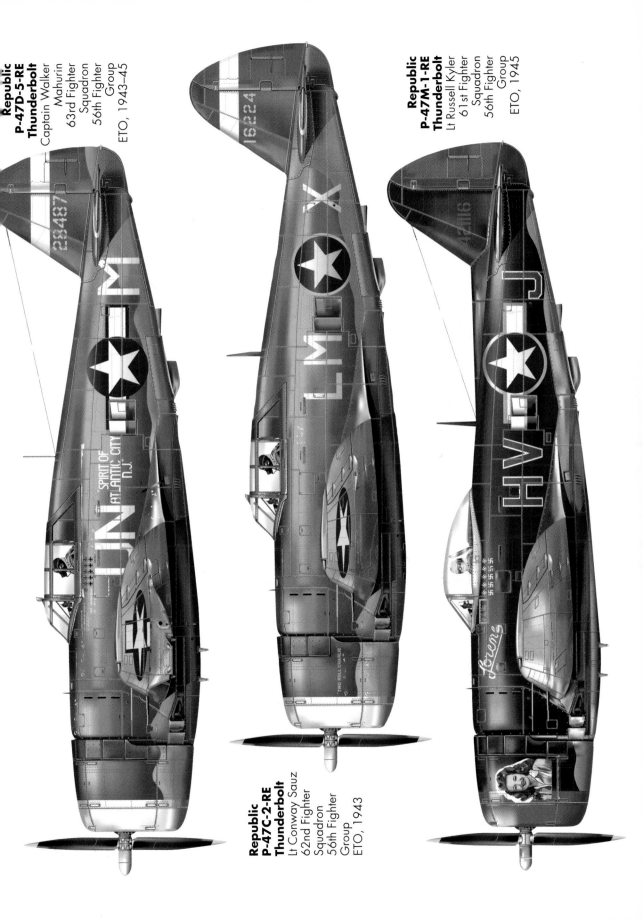

Republic P-47D-5-RE Thunderbolt
Captain Walker Mahurin
63rd Fighter Squadron
56th Fighter Group
ETO, 1943–45

Republic P-47C-2-RE Thunderbolt
Lt Conway Sauz
62nd Fighter Squadron
56th Fighter Group
ETO, 1943

Republic P-47M-1-RE Thunderbolt
Lt Russell Kyler
61st Fighter Squadron
56th Fighter Group
ETO, 1945

Brazil was the largest postwar operator of the P-47 and the fifth-largest in WWII after the US, Britain, France and Russia. This particular D-28, 44-19663, did not take part in the Italian campaign, being allocated on 7 January 1946. After military service with 1o *Grupo de Aviacao de Caca* it was preserved as a monument. (*MAP*)

established on the island of Formosa (Taiwan) in December 1949, the Chinese Nationalist Air Force received enough F-47Ds from the US to equip two squadrons. Other examples reportedly 'switched sides' and flew in Chinese People's Armed Forces Air Force colours. The Chinese, incidentally, followed the US designation system insofar as an initial identification letter 'P' followed by a number was applied to fighters. When US designations changed after the war Chinese Thunderbolts were designated 'F-47' followed by a number.

Colombia

The *Fuerza Aerea Colombiana* took delivery of F-47s in July 1947 and used about 35 to form 1o *Escuadron de Caza*. Flown extensively on training and exercise sorties, the Thunderbolts saw a little action against rebel forces operating in the country's border regions. By May 1953 there were 22 F-47s on strength, but as with many such aircraft in South America serviceability was a problem. The Thunderbolts were replaced by jets two years later.

Cuba

US government credits enabled Cuba to purchase 25 F-47D-30s and -35s which were delivered to the *Fuerza Aerea Ejercito de Cuba* (Cuban Army Air Force) beginning in May 1952. The following year they equipped *Escuadron de Persecucion '10 de Marzo'*, the country's first fighter unit which reportedly had additionally a single TF-47.

Helping to quell an attempt by anti-Batista rebels to topple the government in September 1957, the strength of the *escuadron* had by then fallen to 12 of the ageing Thunderbolts. These survived the war of revolution in 1959 to be 'inherited' by Fidel Castro's *Fuerza Aerea Revolucionaria*. A lack of spares, exacerbated by the US embargo, gradually forced their retirement and replacement by Soviet aircraft during the early 1960s.

Dominican Republic

One of the few countries to buy surplus F-47s from the US rather than accepting them as military aid, the Dominican Republic formed

Postwar French use of the F-47D was quite extensive, and included combat in Algeria in the mid-1950s. This F47D-30 (44-20021), coded 10-SS, belonged to GC III/10. (*MAP*)

the fighters into one large composite unit, the 1o *Escuadron de Caza Bombardero*, in 1953. With 25 F-47D-30s plus a number of other single- and twin-engined types in service, the *Aviacon Militar Dominicana* found this arrangement unwieldy, with consequentially low utilisation of the Thunderbolts. They nevertheless served actively with the AMD until 1957, when they were replaced by jets.

France

Probably expecting to phase out all foreign aircraft sooner than actually occurred, the *Armée de l'Air* found itself using F-47s and other US types for ground attack sorties when it became embroiled in a war in Algeria in 1954. Initially using jets in a counter-insurgency role, it was soon realised that slower piston-engined aircraft were more effective, and the F-47, then being used in combat training units, was recalled to action. Five units (EC 2/6, EEOC 1/17, EC 1/8, EC 1/20 and EC 3/20) used F-47Ds from Oran and Rabat, the Thunderbolts having in some instances occupied these bases since 1951. Usually operated in conjunction with other types in the same parent unit, the F-47 remained in French service until the mid-1960s, serving with a total of 12 first-line and training units.

Iran

When the Imperial Iranian Air Force became independent in August 1955 it formed a single fighter bomber wing with F-47Ds. By that time deliveries via the US had exceeded 50 aircraft, these being used to equip several units. Thunderbolts were deployed on different air bases around the country until 1957–58.

Italy

Italy's none too happy association with the F-47D began in December 1950 with the delivery of 23 out of 100 F-47s allocated. Cold War pressure to have all Western nations equipped with jet fighters could not be achieved overnight and the WWII aircraft were supplied as a stop-gap measure. The *Aeronautica Militare Italiana* formed 20o and 21o *Gruppi* in 51o *Stormo* but a lack of spares meant that only 77 could realistically be used. Poor serviceability and technical problems were largely overcome but accidents were frequent and in 1951, 51o *Stormo* converted to F-84s and passed its Thunderbolts to 5o *Stormo*. In February 1953, 45 F-47s were transferred to 23 *Gruppo Caccia* which in turn relinquished them for overhaul in 1954. These, along with the original 23 aircraft retained for spares, were returned to US depots in Germany in October of that year.

Iranian P-47D-30s lined up at Tehran in July 1949. The country received at least 50 Thunderbolts. (*Olmsted*)

Mexico

Twenty-five refurbished P-47D-35s were transferred to Mexico at the end of 1945. These machines effectively replaced the 25 P-47Ds the Mexicans had used in combat in the Philippines in 1945: five extra backup aircraft were not required and remained in the US. Issued to *Escuadron de Pelea* 201, the numerical designation of the original wartime expeditionary force, the F-47s soldiered on until they were retired in 1957.

Nicaragua

Another country that used the F-47 'in anger', Nicaragua's *Fuerza Aerea* received F-47Ns in 1954. All these came from stocks held by the Puerto Rico Air National Guard and about six were used in Operation *Success*, a CIA-backed invasion to depose Jacabo Arbenz and install Castillo Armas. It was indeed a success and the surviving Thunderbolts, all apparently with a reduced armament of only six machine guns, saw further service with the FAN.

In action again in 1955 the remaining F-47Ns flew the Thunderbolt's last combat sorties. Four years later they were phased out and in 1962

the last three were bought for the Confederate Air Force (CAF).

Peru

ARP-supplied F-47D-30s began arriving in Peru in July 1947, 25 aircraft subsequently entering service with the *Escuadron de Caza* 11. *Esc de Caza 13* was formed in 1953 with 25 F-47D-40s. Between 1953 and 1958 the F-47s provided useful training mounts and by generally overcoming supercharger and other technical troubles the *Fuerza Aerea del Peru* managed to extend their useful life until 1969. This was mainly because no suitable F-47 replacement was available and aircraft were needed to support an F-80 jet training programme. This longevity marked out Peru's Thunderbolts as the last in Latin-American service. Six F-47D-40 survivors were snapped up by the CAF in 1969 and returned to the USA.

Portugal

On formation in July 1952 the *Forca Aerea Portuguesa* acquired 50 F-47D-25s under MDAP. The aircraft were issued in equal numbers to *Esquadra* 10 and 11 and based at Ota. With the

Two of the last six operational Thunderbolts. Purchased by the Confederate Air Force when they became surplus to requirements in Peru in 1969, this 'flight and a half' of Thunderbolts gave a big boost to the US warbird scene at a time when P-47 numbers were at a very low level. This view shows two of the ex-Peruvian aircraft at Harlingen, Texas in November 1970. (*AAHS via Ed Jurist*)

arrival of the first jets in January 1953, all the F-47s were transferred to *Esq* 10 and used for transition training. The unit moved to Tancos that year and existed for another three, the F-84 finally ousting its older stablemate in 1956.

Puerto Rico

Puerto Rico's F-47s were included in the US Air National Guard structure, the 198th Fighter Squadron (Augmented) being established on 23 November 1947. One P-47D-30 was supplied, followed by at least 22 F-47Ns. The unit was mobilised in October 1950 to help quell a riot by prison inmates, a show of force involving a few rounds of Thunderbolt gunfire being enough to bring this about. The 198th was demobilised on 7 November 1954 and had the distinction of being the last unit with official USAF connections to operate the Thunderbolt.

Turkey

About five years before joining NATO, Turkey was already considered by the Alliance as a southern bulwark against Communist expansionism, and military aid was approved by the US Congress in May 1947. Subsequent deliveries of US aircraft included an unknown number of F-47Ds supplied in 1948.

Venezuela

An air arm equipped primarily with trainers, the *Fuerza Aerea Venezolana* took delivery of six F-47Ds under ARP in August 1947. Crashes reduced this to four, one replacement being supplied. In 1949 22 F-47s were delivered to equip *Grupo Aereo* 9 at Maracay. Attrition and a shortage of spares reduced the inventory to about eight F-47s by late 1951, these then being operated by *Escuadron de Casa* No 36 until 1952 when the F-47 was finally phased out.

Yugoslavia

Joining a mixture of Western and Russian types inherited from WWII service, the Yugoslavian air force's fighter arm received about 150 F-47Ds, enough to equip ten first-line squadrons. These MAP-supplied aircraft were regarded as main equipment until they were replaced by jets in 1958. The remaining Thunderbolts were then used as advanced trainers in company with other types, a duty which extended their service until 1961.

Flying as the mount of Glenn Eagleston, with a borrowed serial, this aircraft was one of the ex-Peruvian Air Force P-47Ds acquired by the Confederate Air Force. (*S. Howe*)

Among the P-47s retained by the manufacturers for trials was the first of 550 N-1s, which had high visibility nose and tail markings finished in bright yellow. (*Republic*)

5. Thunderbolt Family: Versions and Variants

P-47B
First production model with short, 35 ft 4.19 in (10.77 m) fuselage and fabric-covered control surfaces; Curtiss Electric propeller.

P-47C-RE
Metal-covered elevators; revised fin design with metal control surfaces; rudder hinge increased overall length by 1 in (2.54 cm); CE propeller.

P-47C-1-RE
Forward fuselage extended by 8 in (20.32 cm) to 36 ft 1.19 in (11.19 m) from aircraft 41-6066; fixed deflection plate on lower fuselage nose between oil cooler shutter and exhaust waste gate; other minor changes.

P-47C-2-RE
Similar to P-47C-1 but with four-point belly shackles for 200-gal (166.5 Imp gal/757 l) ferry tank.

P-47C-5
Similar to P-47C-1 with minor changes; some examples fitted with B-7 belly shackles giving bulged lower fuselage profile.

P-47D
First P-47 built at Evansville, Indiana; similar to P-47C-2.

P-47D-RE
'RE' continues to indicate Farmingdale production; 'RA' suffix introduced to denote manufacture at new Evansville plant.

P-47D-1-RE
Increase in number of cowl flaps to 12 to improve cooling; distinctive 'cut-out' on rear of lower two flaps on each side; additional pilot armour in cockpit; other minor changes.

P-47D-2-RE
Turbo shroud removed; otherwise similar to P-47D-1.

P-47D-2-RA
Similar to P-47D-2.

P-47D-3-RA
Model not to P-47D-5-RE standard – intermediate block number used; similar to P-47D-2-RA.

P-47D-4-RA
Model not to P-47D-5-RE standard – intermediate block number used. Provision for water injection with 15-gal (12.5 Imp gal/56.8 l) tank; GE C-21 supercharger; otherwise similar to P-47D-3-RA.

P-47D-5-RE
First production model with provision for water injection with engine-driven pump. Two-point B-7 bomb shackles installed to take bomb up to 500 lb (227 kg).

P-47D-6-RE
Fuselage store station changed from two-point B-7 to four-point B-10 shackles; otherwise similar to P-47D-1-RE.

P-47D-10-RE

C-23 supercharger; other internal changes. Introduction of cable-charging of guns.

P-47D-11-RE

Electrically driven water pump operated automatically by throttle lever.

P-47D-11-RA

Evansville standardised with Farmingdale; similar model/detail changes.

P-47D-15-RE

Production installation of two wing pylons enabling up to 2,500 lb (1134 kg) of bombs on three stores stations; external tankage increased to 375 US gal (312.3 Imp gal/1420 l); jettisonable canopy.

P-47D-15-RA

Changes as P-47D-15-RE.

P-47D-16-RE

Similar to P-47D-11-RE with detail changes.

P-47D-16-RA

Similar to P-47D-11-RE.

P-47D-20-RE

Engine change to R-2800-59 with GE ignition system; tailwheel leg lengthened; changes to tail of wing pylon; other detail changes; 250th D-20 (42-76614) completed as XP-47L; natural metal finish adopted from 42-25274.

P-47D-20-RA

Similar to P-47D-20-RE.

P-47D-21-RE

Revised throttle quadrant; other minor changes but otherwise similar to P-47D-11-RE.

P-47D-21-RA

Similar to P-47D-11-RE; changes as for P-47D-21-RE.

P-47D-22-RE

First block of P-47s fitted with 13 ft 1.875 in (4.01 m) Hamilton Standard Hydromatic (HSH) cuffless paddle-blade propeller with blunter hub than CE type; overall length extended to 35 ft 10 in (10.92 m).

P-47D-23-RA

First block fitted with 13-ft (3.96 m) Curtiss Electric cuffed paddle-blade propeller; other detail changes.

P-47D-25-RE

First production model P-47 with 360 degree bubble canopy, electrically operated; HSH propeller; water injection tank capacity doubled to 30 US gal (29 Imp gal/132 l) giving maximum duration of 15 minutes; cockpit layout revised; other detail changes.

P-47D-26-RA

Evansville equivalent to P-47D-25 but with CE propeller.

P-47D-27-RE

From 42-27074 power rating was increased by 130 hp with water injection (64 hp without); other changes; batch provided three YP-47Ms and XP-47N.

P-47D-28-RE

CE propeller increased overall length to 36 ft 1 3/4 in (11.02 m); some cockpit controls relocated; changes to hydraulic and radio systems.

P-47D-28-RA

Evansville equivalent to P-47D-28-RE; CE propeller.

P-47D-30-RE

Blunt-nosed ailerons introduced; revised gun-camera mount; elimination of ring-and-bead sight; electric release for external stores; sway braces for stores made permanent; rearview mirror for canopy introduced; CE propeller.

P-47D-30-RA

Evansville output of P-47D-30s exceeded that of all other blocks, running to 1,800 aircraft; similar to P-47D-30-RE; CE propeller.

P-47D-40-RA

Dorsal fin fitted as factory modification; K-14 gunsight; provision for up to ten zero-length launchers (five per wing) for HVARs; CE propeller.

With the pilot pulling up a landing gear that was too long to fit into the wing bays without ingenious compression struts, an early P-47C begins its less than meteoric climb out. (*MAP*)

Three sizeable batches of P-47D-20s were built at both Farmingdale and Evansville. Aircraft 42-25315 was an example of the second batch completed by the parent factory. (*MAP*)

XP-47E
Built as P-47B.

XP-47F
Built as P-47B.

P-47G-CU
First P-47 model built by Curtiss, similar to P-47C-RE. Provision for blind-flying hood on all aircraft; most used as trainers; CE propeller.

P-47G-1-CU
Similar to P-47C-1-RE with 36 ft 1.19 in (11 m) fuselage length.

P-47G-5-CU
Similar to P-47D-1-RE.

P-47G-10-CU
Similar to P-47D-5-RE; two-point B-7 bomb shackles fitted.

P-47G-15-CU
Similar to P-47D-10-RE.

P-47G-16-CU
Two P-47G-15s (42-25267 and 42-25266) experimentally modified as TP-47G two-seaters with main fuel tank reduced in size and second cockpit built above it; front cockpit extended forward with glazed section between both canopies.

XP-47H
One only (42-23297) completed and flown; P-47D-15 (42-23298) allocated for conversion but not completed.

XP-47J
Modified P-47D (43-46952).

XP-47K
One P-47D-5-RE (42-8702) modified with 360 degree bubble canopy.

XP-47L
One P-47D-20 (42-76614) modified with bubble canopy; CE propeller.

YP-47M-RE
Three P-47D-27s (42-27385, '386 and '388) fitted with R-2800 'C' Series engine and new CH-5

turbocharger as forerunners of production P-47M; CE propeller.

P-47M-1-RE
R-2800-57 engine delivering up to 2,800 hp; all examples shipped to UK for use by 56th FG; dorsal fin fitted in theatre; CE propeller.

XP-47N
One P-47D-27-RE (42-27387) extensively modified. Same engine and some engineering similarities to P-47M but with new wing of 22-in (0.56m)-greater span with wider 18 ft 6-in (5.64 m) undercarriage track and four internal fuel cells holding total of 200 US gal (171.9 Imp gal/757 l). Dorsal fin deeper than that fitted to P-47D; CE propeller.

P-47N-1-RE
New cockpit boost/propeller mixture/throttle quadrant; modified wing fuel cells for total 186 US gal (159.8 Imp gal/704 l). Provision for sway braces for 300 gal (257.8 Imp gal/1136 l) drop tanks under each wing panel; CE propeller.

P-47N-5-RE
R-2800-73 engine; installation of zero-length rocket launchers; other detail changes; CE propeller.

P-47N-15-RE
S-1 bomb rack replaced B-10 shackles; K-14A or K-14B gunsight in place of K-14; arm rests for pilot's seat; CE propeller.

P-47N-20-RE
Internal changes only; CE propeller.

P-47N-20-RA
Revised cockpit floor with smooth rudder-pedal track from 45-50051; CE propeller.

P-47N-25-RE
Revised cockpit floor with smooth rudder-pedal track from 44-89294; ailerons and flaps reinforced against rocket blast; CE propeller.

XP-72
Fastest P-47 of entire series; first aircraft (43-6598) flown with four-bladed propeller for Pratt & Whitney R-4360 engine; second (43-6599) with contra-rotating six-blade propeller.

Appendix 1
Weapons and Systems

As with the majority of its US contemporaries, the P-47 relied on a battery of Colt-Browning M2 0.50-in (12.7 mm) machine guns as its main armament. Fired by electrical contact, each gun battery was staggered by about six inches to allow clearance for the belt feeds from the ammunition trays to run inboard over the top of the gun and down into the loading chamber. Each gun had a capacity of between 267 and 425 rounds (increased to 500 in the P-47N) consisting of HE, armour piercing, ball or incendiary.

Weight was always a factor in fighter performance and some combat units strove for an extra few miles per hour by reducing the P-47's guns to six. With all eight guns installed the aircraft had the advantage of offering considerable flexibility in the amount of ammunition carried to save weight. The so-called six-gun 'Superbolt' flown by the 359th Fighter Group achieved some success in combat, primarily against high-flying Bf 109s. Although the idea was not adopted widely by the 8th Air Force other pilots were quite happy to fly with six guns. The 359th had the satisfaction of overcoming one of the P-47's drawbacks which was its inability to climb fast. Stateside training units regularly flew six or four-gun Thunderbolts in the interests of weight saving, performance gain and manoeuvrability.

Gunsights
Although early P-47s had the N-3 reflector sight this did not always operate satisfactorily and from late 1943 Republic fitted the Mk VIII sight in the P-47D-15, which was also of the reflector type. In the interim a British Mk II sight was fitted, all cockpit mountings being backed up by a simple 'ring and post' sight. The Mk VIII sight could be identified by its circular sighting mirror. Alternatively the N-3A reflector sight with a vertical, round-topped mirror could be installed, each sight coming complete with a heavy-duty mounting bracket. The K-14 gyroscopic computing sight was factory-installed on the P-47D-40-RA, the ring and post being eliminated during production of the P-47D-30. The K-14, the 'ace maker' sight, greatly enhanced deflection shooting and was installed on earlier models at depots and bases during overhauls. The derivative K-14A and K-14B sights were fitted to the P-47N.

Cameras
A standard cine-film gun-camera was installed in the P-47. A late-war innovation was to fit a K-24 camera in the cockpit behind the pilot's seat to enable oblique target-strike photos to be obtained.

Bombs
Beefing up the ground attack effort meant fitting high explosive bombs, and the P-47D-15 was the first to be cleared to carry two M-43 500-lb (227 kg) General Purpose or Semi-Armour Piercing bombs on wing racks. The load was increased to a maximum of 1,000 lb (454 kg) per rack by D-Day, bomb types used including the high explosive M-43 GP, the RDX-filled M-65 GP and the M-59 SAP.

The total permissible ordnance load on P-47s often included combinations of GP, armour-piercing, delayed-action bombs and M-81 fragmentation bombs. The latter weighed 20 lb (9 kg) and were carried either in separate 8-round clusters weighing 160 lb (72.6 kg) or were used in combination with larger bombs. 'Frags' were assembled as a load on a bar rack for lifting purposes and attached as a complete unit to the P-47's wing rack.

Rockets
Triple-round 'Bazooka' rocket launchers became part of the P-47's ordnance load shortly after D-Day. A weapon with limited effectiveness from some points of view, the M-10 at least had some 'stand off' capability if used against targets heavily defended by the Thunderbolt's most deadly adversary, light flak. The tubes were attached under each wing in such a way that they were jettisonable in flight (with or without the rockets) – an option some pilots certainly took to reduce the drag of six tubes, especially if their aircraft had suffered a degree of battle damage.

The launchers came in three types – M-10, M-14 and M-15 – and differed only in the material they were constructed from – plastic, steel and magnesium. The plastic tubes were of thicker gauge than the others at 0.25 in and weighed 80 lb (36.3 kg) while the steel tubes were 0.125 in thick weighing 190 lb (86.2 kg) and the magnesium type was 0.19 in thick with a weight of 86 lb (39 kg). All tubes were 10 ft (3 m) long.

Only the M-10 and M-15 tubes were used in combat, the heavier M-14 being reserved for training. The latter also had the deflection arms and straps omitted. All tubes fired a 4.5-in (114 mm) M-8 projectile fitted with an M-4 nose fuze, aiming being by the gunsight as the tubes were bore-sighted with the guns. Firing was singly or in train with 1/10th of a second interval between each.

The total loaded weight of an M-10 triple launcher was 450 lb (204 kg), which clipped 15 to 20 mph (24 to 32 km/h) off the P-47's top speed. This was not really significant and the inherent stability of the aircraft tended to enhance the accuracy of the rockets during firing runs.

Firing trials with British-designed rockets and guide rails were conducted at Wright Field on a P-47D (42-8053) but were not officially adopted for combat by either the USAAF or RAF. After numerous aircraft had used them operationally rails were found to have been so much surplus weight, hence the widespread adoption of light and convenient zero-length launchers. They were also more efficient than the triple tube launchers. Stubs to take up to ten HVARs (High Velocity Air Rockets) were factory-fitted on the P-47D-40 and three P-47N production blocks, the N-5, N-20 and N-25.

A full load of HVARs on the maximum five pairs of launchers was tested on the P-47N but this number of rockets is not known to have been widely used in combat, if at all, since they would have prevented the use of drop tanks.

Mixed loads were usually carried in the Pacific where the already heavy P-47N had also, on occasion, to allow for the carriage of bombs. Up to four pairs of launchers were positioned between the wing racks and the undercarriage legs. Standard HE and shaped-charge anti-armour heads were used.

Napalm

Drop tanks filled with a jellied petrol substance in crystal form detonated by a thermite grenade – or gunfire once they had been dropped – were the first napalm or fire bombs. These were also referred to as napalm-gel fire bombs. Used in most war theatres, these makeshift napalm bombs were usually very effective. Napalm generates extremely intense heat, making it effective against lighter structures such as those made of wood.

There were several novel approaches to obtaining napalm-type bombs for P-47s before they were issued officially. An example based on the 108-gal (92.8

Imp gal/408.8 l) fuel tank was invented by Glenn Duncan of the 353rd Group. Filled with gasoline and oil the 'Duncan Cocktail' had an M-14 incendiary grenade as an igniter. Two external grenade igniters gave a variation on the theme.

Smoke tanks

The distinctive M-10 and M-33 chemical tanks could be installed on most USAAF fighters, the P-47D being no exception. Designed to lay down a chemical or tear-gas spray or smoke screens from low altitude, the tanks were adapted from standard fuel tanks and could be attached to the wing pylons.

The early M-10 was similar to a 75-gal (64.5 Imp gal/284 l) 'teardrop' P-47 belly tank, fitted with a pump and a ventral ejector nozzle to disperse the chemical downwards and behind the aircraft.

The M-33 had a cylindrical container, based on a shortened 108-gal (92.8 Imp gal/408.8 l) fuel tank, which terminated roughly in line with the aft end of the wing pylon. An ejector nozzle similar to that of the M-10 was fitted.

As far as the P-47 was concerned both the M-10 and M-33 were tested but neither appears to have had any operational use. The 56th Fighter Group's P-47Ms were fitted out for a smoke-screening of German flak units in 1945, but the end of the war meant that the idea was not tried in action.

Special weapons

By investing heavily in the 50-calibre machine-gun as a standard aircraft weapon, the US did not specify cannon armament for fighters in anywhere near the numbers favoured by European designers. Air chiefs were nevertheless aware of the superior penetrating/explosive power of cannon shells over machine-gun ammunition, and some operational tests were carried out. In 1944 the P-47D was selected to field-test a 20-mm Hispano cannon manufactured under licence by Oldsmobile.

Selected P-47Ds of the 8th Air Force's 78th FG had a single unfaired gun (fairings were apparently made but not fitted) complete with its drum magazine attached to each wing rack. The assembly weighed only 102 lb (46.25 kg) complete, which was light enough, but installing internal cannon would have demanded considerable wing modification. Had operational guns occupied wing racks as tested the aircraft would have lost its main ordnance carriage so in the event, no change was made to the Thunderbolt's gun calibre while hostilities lasted.

Appendix 2
Specifications

XP-47
Type: single-seat fighter (prototype)
Powerplant: One 2,000 hp Pratt & Whitney R-2800-17/-35 18-cylinder two-row radial
Dimensions:

span	40 ft 9 in (12.42 m)
length	35 ft 4 in (10.77 m)
height	14 ft 2 in (4.32 m)
wing area	300 sq ft (27.87 m²)

Weights:

empty	9,189 lb (4168 kg)
loaded	12,700 lb (5761 kg)

Performance:

maximum speed	412 mph (663 km/h)
service ceiling	36,000 ft (10900 m)
range	575 miles (925 km) at 25,000 ft (7620 m)

Armament:
provision for 8 x 0.50-in MGs with 500 rounds per gun (rpg)

P-47C-1
Type: single-seat fighter
Powerplant: One 2,000 hp Pratt & Whitney R-2800-21
Dimensions:

span	40 ft 9 5/16 in (12.43 m)
length	36 ft 1 3/16 in (11 m)
height	14 ft 3 5/16 in (4.35 m)
wing area	330 sq ft (30.66 m²)

Weights:

empty	9,900 lb (4491 kg)
loaded	13,500 lb (6123 kg)

Performance:

maximum speed	420 mph (676 km/h)
service ceiling	42,000 ft (12800 m)
max range	835 miles (1344 km)

Armament:
6 or 8 x 0.50-in machine guns with up to 425 rpg

P-47D-10
Type: single-seat fighter bomber
Powerplant: One 2,000 hp Pratt & Whitney R-2800-63
Dimensions:

span	40 ft 9 5/16 in (12.43 m)
length	36 ft 1 3/16 in (11 m)
height	14 ft 3 5/16 in (4.35 m)
wing area	300 sq ft (27.87 m²)

Weights:

empty	9,900 lb (4491 kg)
loaded	13,500 lb (6123 kg)

Performance:

maximum speed	433 mph (697 km/h)
service ceiling	42,000 ft (12800 m)
max range	825 miles (1328 km)

Armament:
As for P-47C

P-47D-30
Type: single-seat fighter bomber
Powerplant: One 2,000/2,430 hp Pratt & Whitney R-2800-59
Dimensions:

span	40 ft 9 5/16 in (12.43 m)
length	36 ft 1 3/4 in (11.02 m)
height	14 ft 8 1/16 in (4.47 m)

Weights:

empty	10,000 lb (4536 kg)
loaded	14,500 lb (6577 kg)

Performance:

maximum speed	423 mph (681)
service ceiling	42,000 ft (12800 m)
range	1,030 miles (1658 km)

Armament:
8 machine guns, as for other variants, plus up to 2,500 lb (1134 kg) of bombs

P-47N-20
Type: single-seat fighter bomber
Powerplant: One 2,100/2,800 hp Pratt & Whitney R-2800-73/77
Dimensions:

span	42 ft 6 5/16 in (12.96 m)
length	36 ft 1 3/4 in (11.02 m)
height	14 ft 6 in (4.42 m)
wing area	322.2 sq ft (29.94 m²)

Weights:

empty	10,988 lb (4984 kg)
loaded	13,823 lb (6270 kg)
maximum	21,200 lb (9616 kg)

Performance:

maximum speed	467 mph (752 km/h)
service ceiling	43,000 ft (13110 m)
normal range	800 miles (1287 km);
maximum range	2,000 miles (3219 km)

Armament:
Similar to P-47D but up to 500 rounds per gun; provision for ten zero-length HVAR launchers. Some aircraft carried M-10 triple-round launchers in place of fewer HVARs

Notes:
XP-47H
As for P-47D-15 except: length 38 ft 4 in (11.68 m); empty weight 11,442 lb (5190 kg); loaded weight 14,010 lb (6355 kg); top speed 414 mph (666 km/h); ceiling 37,700 ft (11490 m)

XP-72
As for P-47D-40 except: powerplant one 3,000 hp Pratt & Whitney R-4360-13; length 36 ft 11 in (11.25 m); empty weight 10,965 lb (4974 kg) loaded 14,750 lb (6690 kg); maximum speed 490 mph (788 km/h)

Appendix 3
P-47 Production

Building a total of 15,683 P-47s involved three main plants – Republic at Farmingdale on Long Island and Evansville, Indiana which opened in 1942, and Curtiss at its Buffalo plant in New York. Farmingdale completed 9,087 and Evansville 6,242, with Curtiss additionally building 354 P-47Gs. With the termination of production 5,934 additional P-47Ns were cancelled.

Faced with meeting the largest order the Air Corps had ever placed for a fighter, Republic's main plant (known as Building 17) rose to the challenge well and completed 171 P-47Bs by the spring of 1942.

Not surprisingly the Japanese attack on Pearl Harbor on 7 December 1941 galvanised the nation. The feeling of outrage and a burning desire to strike back at the Axis was taken up with a will by the aircraft industry, and at Republic employees clubbed together to build a P-47 and present it to the government without charge. This aircraft, P-47B (41-5901) dubbed *Lucky Seven! Gift of the Republic Aviation Employees*, was the forerunner of other Thunderbolts donated by company employees. Others were paid for by war bond drives and state, county and organisational donations.

Each aircraft carried a suitable inscription on the fuselage – for example P-47D-1

Jackson County Michigan Fighter, (42-7877), P-47D-25 *Oregon's Britannia* (42-26413) and P-47D-5 *Spirit of Atlantic City, NJ* (42-8487). All these T-bolts saw service with the 56th Fighter Group and all were flown by 8th Air Force aces. Several less-well-documented subscription P-47s are known including P-47D-2 *Collingdale PA* (42-8304) and P-47D-10 (42-74986) bought by New York financiers and appropriately named *Rockville Center Bankers*.

These 'War Bond Planes' as they were known, carried either a painted fuselage inscription or an oval design with a Republic logo and number, presumably applied as a decal. Out of at least 65 razorback and bubbletop D models known to have been purchased with bonds the second was a D-22 (44-260046) named *Fightin' Gator* which saw service in the 404th FG, 9th Air Force. In this and other instances the inscription was treated with respect and allowed to remain even to the extent of compromising unit markings. War Bond Plane No 32 was another P-47D-22 (42-26088) which went to the CBI and was flown by the 81st FG. Number 65 was 42-27275, a D-27 of the 365th Group, 9th Air Force.

In a different category were the production milestone Thunderbolts carrying inscriptions

to denote the fact that they were the 1,000th, 5,000th, 10,000th and 15,000th examples off the line. Three shifts were soon required to build P-47s 'around the clock' at Farmingdale and by March 1942 when the first P-47B rolled out, the production rate was rising towards a summer goal of 50 aircraft a month. This was reached and surpassed to meet accelerated orders for subsequent models. Due to this demand Republic experienced some delays, however, and by early 1944 a two-month slippage in allocation of completed airframes persisted for some months.

By the end of 1944 the company had 24,450 employees, 30 per cent of whom were women. An expanding work-force had steadily reduced both the man-hours required to complete a P-47 and the unit cost to the Army. Building the first 773 aircraft had required an average of 22,925 man-hours but at the point that the last rivet was put into *Ten Grand* only 6,290 man-hours had been required to complete the aircraft. The cost of a single P-47 had concurrently dropped from an average $68,750 to $45,600. P-47Ns continued to pour off the line as the end of WWII came and went but in December 1945, the wartime production tap could finally be turned off.

Production of Thunderbolts broke down as follows:		
XP-47B	**P-47D-6-RE**	**P-47D-25-RE**
1 (40-3051)	350 (42-74615 to 42-74964)	385 (42-26389 to 42-26773)
P-47B	**P-47D-10-RE**	**P-47D-26-RA**
171 (41-5895 to 41-6065)	250 (42-74965 to 42-75214)	250 (42-28189 to 28438)
P-47C-RE	**P-47D-11-RE**	**P-47D-27-RE**
57 (41-6067 to 41-6123)	400 (42-75215 to 42-75614)	615 (42-26774 to 42-27388)
P-47C-1-RE	**P-47D-11-RA**	**P-47D-28-RE**
55 (41-6066 & 41-6124 to 41-6177)	250 (42-22864 to 42-23113)	750 (44-19558 to 44-20307)
P-47C-2-RE	**P-47D-15-RE**	**P-47D-28-RA**
128 (41-6178 to 41-6305)	496 (42-75615 to 42-75864 & 42-76119 to 42-76364)	1,028 (42-28439 to 42-29466)
P-47C-5-RE	**P-47D-15-RA**	**P-47D-30-RE**
362 (41-6306 to 41-6667)	157 (42-23143 to 42-23299)	800 (44-20308 to 44-21107)
P-47D	**P-47D-16-RE**	**P-47D-30-RA**
4 (42-22250 to 42-22253)	254 (42-75865 to 42-76118)	1,800 (44-32668 to 44-33867 & 44-89684 to 44-90283)
P-47D-RE	**P-47D-16-RA**	**P-47D-40-RA**
110 (42-22254 to 42-22363)	29 (42-23114 to 42-23142)	665 (44-90284 to 44-90483 & 45-49090 to 45-49554)
P-47D-1-RE	**P47D-20-RE**	**XP-47E**
105 (42-7853 to 42-7957)	300 (42-76365 to 42-76614 & 42-25274 to 42-25322)	1 (41-6065)
P-46D-2-RE	**P-47D-20-RA**	**XP-47F**
445 (42-7958 to 42-8402)	187 (43-25254 to 43-25440)	1 (41-5938)
P-47D-2-RA	**P-47D-21-RE**	**P-47G-CU**
200 (42-22364 to 42-22563)	216 (42-25323 to 42-25538)	20 (42-24920 to 42-24939)
P-47D-5-RE	**P-47D-21-RA**	**P-47G-1-CU**
300 (42-8403 to 42-8702)	224 (43-25441 to 43-25664)	40 (42-24940 to 42-24979)
P-47D-3-RA	**P-47D-22-RE**	**P-47G-5-CU**
100 (42-22564 to 42-22663)	850 (42-25539 to 42-26388)	60 (42-24980 to 42-25039)
P-47D-4-RE	**P-47D-23-RA**	**P-47G-10-CU**
200 (42-22664 to 42-22863)	889 (43-25665 to 43-25753 & 42-27389 to 42-28188)	80 (42-25040 to 42-25119)
		P-47G-15-CU

154 (42-25120 to 42-25273)	
XP-47H	
2 (42-23297 and 42-23298)	
XP-47J	
1 (43-46952)	
XP-47K	
1 (42-8702)	
XP-47L	
1 (42-76614)	
YP-47M-RE	
3 (42-27385, 42-27386 & 42-27388)	
P-47M-1-RE	
130 (44-21108 to 44-21237)	
XP-47N	
1 (42-27387)	
P-47N-1-RE	
550 (44-87784 to 44-88333)	
P-47N-5-RE	
550 (44-88334 to 44-88883)	
P-47N-15-RE	
200 (44-88884 to 89083)	
P-47N-20-RE	
200 (44-89084 to 44-89283)	
P-47N-20-RA	
149 (45-49975 to 45-50123)	
P-47N-25-RE	
167 (44-89284 to 44-89450)	
XP-72	
2 (43-6598 and 43-6599)	

Appendix 4
Museum Aircraft and Survivors

US P-47s

In view of its high fuel consumption the P-47 was understandably less attractive than other surplus military aircraft offered to the civilian buyer by the War Assets Administration. To buyers who sought a fast, economical runabout, the fuel bills for a P-47 would have seemed exorbitant, worse than for any other fighter type.

With no continuing large-scale first-line use by the USAF – as was enjoyed by the P-51 in Korea – late-model Thunderbolts were passed to the Air National Guard or scrapped. Eventually their numbers dwindled to the point where one of America's most important combat aircraft seemed in danger of extinction.

Things grew so bad in this regard that even Republic had difficulty in locating a complete airframe to fly in the aircraft's 20th anniversary celebrations in 1961. The manufacturer's employees were met by blank stares when they requested the Air Force to 'draw a P-47 from storage'.

Eventually a razorback D-15 model (42-23278) latterly registered N5087V and N347D was found by Bob Bean at Blyth, California. The company purchased the intact but neglected aircraft and after refurbishment, exhibited it at numerous air shows to a highly enthusiastic reception.

As insurance, Republic also borrowed a bubbletop P-47D-30 (44-32691) owned by the Air & Space Museum and painted it with a 20th Anniversary logo. This was posed alongside the then current company product, the F-105D Thunderchief.

Sent to Europe in 1963 the razorback Thunderbolt performed at the Paris Air Show and events in England where the type had not been seen in the air for 20 years. Having been put through its paces in front of thousands of people, the aircraft was retired in 1964 after being badly damaged in an accident. It was subsequently repaired and donated to the USAF Museum, where it resides today in honourable retirement, a fitting monument to the thousands of young American and Allied airmen who flew Thunderbolts in WWII. The fact that the aircraft is a rare razorback model made it all the more significant, for elsewhere the bubbletop variety predominated.

The appearance of a P-47 on the air show display circuit was an event that helped kick-start the previously moribund preservation movement which gathered momentum throughout the 1960s. Amazingly, when one considers that the aircraft was built in the largest numbers of all US single-seat fighters, such a revival was almost too late for the P-47, particularly the early-production models. Razorbacks had become the ultimate rara avis, and few survived the mass scrapping of the early postwar years.

Then came the Confederate Air Force, dedicated not only to averting the danger of extinction but to 'keeping 'em flying'. Aiming to preserve at least one flying example of every WWII combat aircraft used by American forces was, even in a huge country seemingly littered with examples of old military aircraft, quite a daunting task. Nevertheless a P-47N-15 (44-88436/N47TB) was part of the original collection, this being one of seven complete airframes extant today. Among them is a Lackland AFB exhibit, P-47N-25 (44-89348). Earl Reinert's Victory Air Museum in Illinois rescued the first YP-47M-RE (42-27385/N4477N) after an abortive air racing career. Entered as number 42 in the 1947 Bendix race from Los Angeles to Cleveland, the aircraft suffered a fuel tank leak and had to retire.

Thunderbolts abroad

P-47Ds may have become rare in the US by the 1960s but overseas the picture was a little more encouraging. In the early 1970s six airframes were located in Peru. Recently retired from service with the air force, all were acquired and ferried back to the CAF's main base, then located at Harlingen in Texas. After some years of refurbishing work this Thunderbolt mini-squadron emerged as fully fledged, complete with authentic wartime combat markings representing aircraft in various war theatres. An evocative flypast was staged by CAF pilots in 1974 and since then, notwithstanding a few casualties, these aircraft have formed a core part of an outstanding collection. The P-47s, operated by the various CAF Wings around the US, are regularly repainted in some of the more exotic colour schemes worn in WWII.

South America still boasts a numerically strong collection of P-47s, there being today at least seven in Brazil, two in Bolivia and single examples in Chile, Colombia and Venezuela. Those on permanent display in aviation museums are unlikely to be removed although the continent has long been a rich source of surplus wartime vintage US aircraft and more will undoubtedly return to their native country. A pool of expert restorers exists in North America and it makes sense for organisations and individuals to have such work carried out there.

Today any P-47 carcass discovered in a hitherto unknown backwater should be appreciated for what it once represented and if possible, refurbished or used in some way to keep others flying. At Duxford, Cambridgeshire the Fighter Collection's hybrid P-47D ('42-2667') is a fine example of what can be achieved from a composite rebuild. Constructed from parts of several other P-47s, the aircraft flies appropriately in the colours of the 78th Fighter Group which was so closely associated with the airfield during the war years.

Other P-47s have been rescued from their 'final' resting places such as the D-2 raised from the New Guinea swamp into which it plunged in 1944. Discovered in 1968 it was subsequently restored in New Zealand. Papua New Guinea and the Pacific islands are a veritable treasure trove of military aircraft and for those examples that have been purchased, restoration has saved them for posterity. In recent times the PNG government has placed embargoes on the removal of such relics, arguing that they should be left in situ as monuments. But such a policy, while seemingly laudable, has not prevented deterioration and in some cases destruction.

Neverthless old airframes in the 'basket case' category will certainly continue to provide the raw material for the many dedicated restorers who perform minor miracles in getting a forlorn heap of remains back together, if not in the air again. With about 50 examples remaining in flying condition or as static museum exhibits, the 2003 world inventory of Thunderbolts cannot be called large. But compared with some aircraft produced in high volume during WWII that have since become totally extinct, or have been reduced to a single survivor, that figure is quite encouraging.

Appendix 5
P-47 Models

The P-47 has natural appeal as a model kit subject, all the established manufacturers having added razorback and/or bubbletop versions in all the most popular scales. Depending on the scale, accuracy has varied across the three basic variants, the two D models and the N. The P-47M, externally little different to its late D model parent, has recently been added to a neat Revell 1/72nd scale range of WWII fighters. This is the best bubbletop P-47 to appear in this scale and as well as having wide open engine cowling gills, easily closed by finger pressure, it may be built quickly and finished as any late-war P-47D. Unsurprisingly the kit decals are for aircraft of the 56th Fighter Group.

A good early-model T-bolt equivalent in 1/72 scale may be made from the Matchbox kit, which has an excellent razorback profile – but its many detail faults need rectifying. Mixing and matching parts from other 1/72 P-47 kits is one way to achieve a convincing model.

In general, the P-47 has lent itself to being replicated much better in 1/48th than other scales. Quality offerings from all the 'big names' – Hasegawa, Revell, Tamiya and Academy among others – are all superbly moulded kits containing everything the modeller will need to produce a highly detailed replica. Inevitably perhaps, each has detail faults which are correctable; after-sales accessories for the P-47 abound and more accurate instrument boards, rudder pedals, harness buckles, etc can be added in etched brass and resin.

Of the above kits the writer rates the Hasegawa P-47D-30/40 high in any 'top five' and for the P-47N

the Academy model beats the rest. A very colourful model subject with many operational aircraft having sported delightfully risqué nose art, the P-47N has few equals. Academy reproduced the dorsal fin better than the other kits in this scale and the moulding is superb. The finely detailed component parts extend to external stores and 'round' and 'flattened' wheels with nicely treaded tyres.

Decal manufacturers have noted the vast, multi-theatre possibilities of the P-47 as a scale subject, the field being led by the prolific US firm AeroMaster. The company has extended its single-sheet range to include several themed sets including two covering 20 aircraft of the 405th Fighter Group. These 'specials' include much useful data as well as a photograph of each subject aircraft, which is most welcome.

In 1/32nd scale, Revell is the only firm to date to release kits of the P-47D in both razorback and bubbletop form. These are well worth acquiring but a considerable amount of remedial work is necessary. The long list should run to revising the fin/rudder and cowling lip shapes and adding detail to most other areas such as the wing racks, the propeller, engine access panels, wheels and so on. Of the two, the razorback's canopy is just about usable but the P-47D-25 really needs its poorly moulded bubbletop replaced by a vacuformed item. No USAAF stores were provided in either kit but a vacuform set of drop tanks was marketed by Horizon Conversions of Canada at about the time these kits appeared. Otherwise P-51s and other 1/32nd scale kits will be able to provide some of the necessary drop tanks, bombs and other stores.

Appendix 6
P-47 Books

Anon
The Pratt & Whitney Aircraft Story;
Connecticut, 1950

Bodie, Warren M.
P-47 Thunderbolt;
Widewing Publications, Georgia, 1994

Craven, W.F. & Cate, J.L.
The Army Air Forces in World War II (various volumes)
Office of Air Force History, Washington,1983

Dean, Francis H.
America's One Hundred Thousand: The US Production
of Fighter Aircraft in WWII
Schiffer, Atglen, Pennsylvania, 1997

Freeman, Roger A.
Thunderbolt: a documentary history of the
Republic P-47
MacDonald & Janes, London, 1978

Freeman, Roger A.
The Mighty Eighth War Manual
Jane's, London, 1984

Freeman, Roger A.
56th Fighter Group
Osprey Elite 2, Osprey Publishing, Oxford, 2000

Hagedorn, Daniel P.
Republic P-47 Thunderbolt, The Final Chapter
Phalanx, Minnesota, 1978

Hagedorn, Daniel P.
Central American and Caribbean Air Forces;
Air-Britain, Tonbridge, 1993

Hess, William N.
America's Aces in a Day
Specialty Press, Minnesota, 1996

Johnson, Frederick A.
Republic P-47 Thunderbolt
WarbirdTech 23, Specialty Press, MN, 1999

Scutts, Jerry
Republic P-47 Thunderbolt: the operational record
Airlife Publishing, Shrewsbury, 1998

Scutts, Jerry
P-47 Aces of the Eighth Air Force;
Aircraft of the Aces 24, Osprey Publishing, Oxford, 1998

Scutts, Jerry
P-47 Aces of the Ninth & Fifteenth Air Forces
Aircraft of the Aces 30, Osprey Publishing, Oxford, 1999

Stanaway, John
Mustang & Thunderbolt Aces of the Pacific and CBI
Aircraft of the Aces 26, Osprey Publishing, Oxford, 1999

Stoff, Joshua
The Thunder Factory: an illustrated history of the
Republic Aviation Corporation
Arms and Armour, London, 1990

Index

Page numbers in *italics* refer to illustrations.